LOS ANGELES DISTRICT ATTORNEY
BUREAU OF INVESTIGATION

Hodel-Black Dahlia
Case File No. 30-1268

CONFIDENTIAL TRANSCRIPTS

Containing the official, unabridged, 1950 law-enforcement Electronic Surveillance Recordings of Dr. George Hill Hodel's secret conversations in which he confessed to: police pay-offs, performing illegal abortions and having committed the 1945 murder of his personal secretary, Ruth Spaulding, as well as the 1947 torture-murder of Elizabeth "Black Dahlia" Short. These transcripts also contain the assault, beating and probable real-time murder of a woman—as recorded by detectives during their actual 1950 police stakeout.

STEVE HODEL
New York Times Bestselling Author of *Black Dahlia Avenger*

Thoughtprint Press

LOS ANGELES, CALIFORNIA

This publication is dedicated to three honest cops who lived, worked and tried to do the right thing during one of Los Angeles' most corrupt decades—1940-1950

In Memory of:
Charles Stoker, Sergeant LAPD Vice Squad
Walter Morgan, Investigator, LADA Bureau of Investigation
Frank Jemison, Lieutenant, LADA Bureau of Investigation

Contents

Author's Preface

THE DA'S HODEL-BLACK DAHLIA TRANSCRIPTS

As you begin to read the following summaries, It is important to understand that the detective's entries that make-up these 146-pages of transcriptions are nothing more than *their personal log*. In these files, [with a few fortunate exceptions] we are only reading brief "headlines" as to what was contained in each of the separately recorded conversations.

The officers entries, made in real time, summarize only *bits and pieces* of each conversation. Consequently, we are only receiving a few sentences of a total conversation.

Unfortunately, the actual 41 wire recordings have "disappeared" from LAPD custody, and it is almost certain that the missing recordings containing the complete conversations were destroyed and will never become available.

It is also important to understand that the modern day LAPD had nothing to do with the original investigation *and had no idea that Dr. George Hill Hodel was ever named as a suspect, let alone that he had confessed on tape to committing the crimes. Today's LAPD first learned of both Dr. George Hodel's existence and these transcripts only AFTER the publication of BDA in 2003.*

Today's LAPD had no knowledge that these DA Transcripts existed. All of the evidence connecting George Hodel to the crimes as well as these transcripts was removed from LAPD files a long time ago, probably in the 1950s or 1960s.

Like, LASO Undersheriff, James Downey had told his Chief of Detectives, Gordon Bowers, when speaking about George Hodel and LAPD solving the case, **"...it will never come out."**

Also, keep in mind as you read these transcripts that we owe their existence solely to one honest [and very cautious] detective.

It was Lt. Frank B. Jemison who was assigned by the 1949 Grand Jury to reinvestigate the Black Dahlia and other *Lone Woman Murders*. He did it, and he solved it. When he was then ordered by his superiors to "shut it down and turn over all the files, tape recordings and transcripts to LAPD's Chief of Detectives, Thad Brown, he did that too.

But, it was Lt. Jemison's final act that changed the course of history and permitted the public to ultimately discover the truth.

Prior to turning over all the materials to LAPD, as ordered, Lt. Jemison made a copy of his complete investigation, including the Hodel transcripts, and secretly locked all of the documents away in the DA's vault, where they remained unopened and untouched for six-decades. This was his insurance. Unbeknownst to all the top brass in both the DA's office and the LAPD, *Lt. Jemison kept a second set of books.*

Here then, thanks to an honest and careful cop, are those books!

In the summary pages that follow I have reduced the original 146-page transcript down to just 15 pages for easier readability. Included in those pages are extracts of what I consider to be the most relevant statements and admissions along with my personal notations.

For historical purposes and the hardcore researchers, [and in case I have missed something that an eagle-eyed armchair detective might find] *the complete unedited Hodel- Black Dahlia Transcripts follow and are reproduced here exactly as they were copied from the original 146-pages.*

I have also included Chapter 9, *DA Investigators Jemison and Morgan* from my earlier publication, *Black Dahlia Avenger II* (Thoughtprint Press 2012) so that my readers may have a complete historical understanding of the critical role each of these two lawmen played in the original investigation, and in Morgan's case, his resurfacing and very active role in my 2002 investigation, *some fifty-years later.*

Finally, I will also include the six-page transcript Lt. Frank Jemison conducted with my mother on March 22, 1950, which was the direct cause of my father's immediate flight from the U.S. to avoid arrest and prosecution—*just five days later.*

Annotated 15-page Summary:
Hodel Black Dahlia D.A. Transcripts

LOS ANGELES DISTRICT ATTORNEY

BUREAU OF INVESTIGATION

HODEL – BLACK DAHLIA CASE FILE

ELECTRONIC SURVEILLANCE TRANSCRIPTS OF GEORGE HILL HODEL M.D.

DA Case No. 30-1268
Title- Elizabeth Short
Suspect: Dr. George Hill Hodel
Inv. Assigned: Lt. Frank Jemison
Charge: Murder
Case: ACTIVE

The following fifteen-page annotated summary was prepared by retired LAPD Homicide detective Steve Hodel. It contains the verbatim statements and entries of both DA and LAPD detectives as found in the original 1950 DA Case File.

The statements and admissions made by Dr. George Hill Hodel are also verbatim, taken from the pages of the DA's transcription of the secret wire-recordings.

The tape-recordings were obtained during a joint DA/LAPD Task-Force stakeout comprised of 18 detectives. The electronic surveillance was ongoing 24/7 over a five-week period from February 15, 1950 through March 27, 1950 (1872 man hours) and was terminated only because Dr. Hodel after being tipped-off then fled his residence.

As of that date, detectives had recorded 41 wire spools of Dr. Hodel's personal conversations. The DA's original summary resulted in 146-pages of transcription. In the pages that follow, I have left the original timeline intact, and included only those statements relevant to criminal activity, payoffs to law enforcement, and which make specific references to the Black Dahlia Murder investigation. *The complete and unedited 146-page transcript is included as an addendum to this book.*

2

ELECTRONIC SURVEILLANCE INSTALLATION
DR. GEORGE HILL HODEL RESIDENCE —5121 FRANKLIN AVE, HOLLYWOOD
2/15/50

D.A. Hodel/Black Dahlia File

"INVESTIGATOR'S PROGRESS REPORT"

The handwritten report (above) is a copy of the one found in the D.A. Hodel – Black Dahlia File.

The verbatim typewritten copy at the right includes all spellings and punctuations as they appear in the above original.

Case No. 30-1268   Date: 2/27/50
Title: Short, Eliz.
Suspects: Dr. Geo. Hill   Inv. Assigned Jemison
Charge: Murder
THIS CASE IS: ACTIVE
BRIEF STATEMENT AS TO RESULTS TO DATE: (Indicate present status if being brought to trial at this time.)

"On Feb. 15, 1950 the undersigned investigator, working with Sgts Stanton & Guinnis from the LAPD crime lab, installed two microfones in the home of Dr. Geo. Hodel. The microfones were connected to a wire recorder located in the basement of the Hollywood Station of the LAPD thru telephone lines leased from the Pac. Tel. & Tel. Co. Trouble was not rectified until approx. 2:00, Feb. 18. No intelligible conversation was heard over the system until that time."

Signed—David E. Bronson

DA/LAPD MICROPHONE INSTALLATION LOCATIONS

Two microphone (M) "bugs" installed in main level walls of Dr. Hodel's residence. Based on surveillance transcripts we know they were hidden in the West Office Library, and Master Bedroom. Because of its placement. the bug in George Hodel's bedroom was able to pick-up and record the Feb. 18 assault and possible murder that occurred in the basement. Below floor plan diagrams basement which was located directly below the Master bedroom.

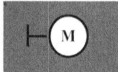

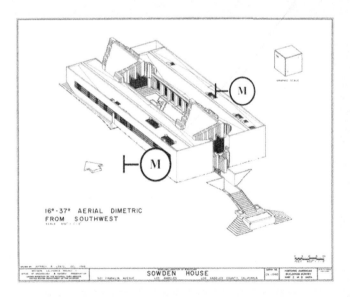

16°-37° AERIAL DIMETRIC
FROM SOUTHWEST

SOWDEN HOUSE

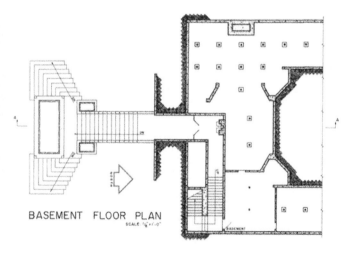

BASEMENT FLOOR PLAN

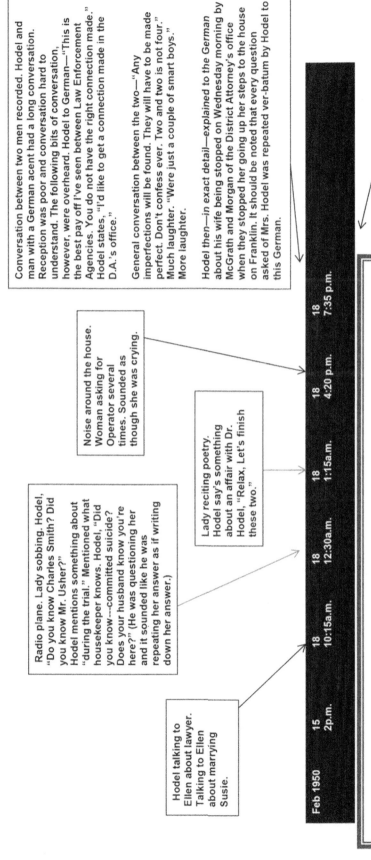

Conversation between two men recorded. Hodel and man with a German accent had a long conversation. Reception was poor and conversation hard to understand. The following bits of conversation, however, were overheard. Hodel to German—"This is the best pay off I've seen between Law Enforcement Agencies. You do not have the right connection made." Hodel states, "I'd like to get a connection made in the D.A.'s office."

General conversation between the two—"Any imperfections will be found. They will have to be made perfect. Don't confess ever. Two and two is not four." Much laughter. "Were just a couple of smart boys." More laughter.

Hodel then—in exact detail—explained to the German about his wife being stopped on Wednesday morning by McGrath and Morgan of the District Attorney's office when they stopped her going up her steps to the house on Franklin. It should be noted that every question asked of Mrs. Hodel was repeated ver-batum by Hodel to this German.

He (Hodel) then began to explain to the German about his recent trial—making statements that, "There'e out to get me. Two men in the D.A.'s officer were transferred and demoted because of my trial." Hodel then explained about his being questioned at the D.A.'s office on Wednesday morning and told in great detail as to questions perpounded to him at that time. One statement made to the German was as follows: "Supposin' I did kill the Black Daliah. They couldn't prove it now. They can't talk to my Secretary anymore because she's dead.....One point of the conversation was also, "Have you heard from Powers.""

Noise around the house. Woman asking for Operator several times. Sounded as though she was crying.

Radio plane. Lady sobbing. Hodel, "Do you know Charles Smith? Did you know Mr. Usher?" Hodel mentions something about "during the trial." Mentioned what housekeeper knows. Hodel, "Did you know—committed suicide? Does your husband know you're here?" (He was questioning her and it sounded like he was repeating her answer as if writing down her answer.)

Lady reciting poetry. Hodel say's something about an affair with Dr. Hodel, "Relax, Let's finish these two."

Hodel talking to Ellen about lawyer. Talking to Ellen about marrying Susie.

Feb 1950	15 2p.m.	18 10:15a.m.	18 12:30a.m.	18 1:15a.m.	18 4:20 p.m.	18 7:35 p.m.

AUTHOR NOTES

[Boxed statements are verbatim as they appear on original transcripts including spelling errors]

Feb. 15- Police microphones installed while Dr. Hodel is being questioned by detectives at the DA detectives downtown office at the Hall of Justice. DA investigator Walter Morgan shims locked front door of Hodel residence and sound technicians place two microphones inside the walls in library and master bedroom.

Charles Smith, referred to above, was an abortionist friend of Hodel's and in Sept. 1949, assisted in the abortion of his 14-year-old daughter, Tamar. Smith and a Dr. Francis C. Ballard were arrested by LAPD just days after Dr. Hodel's arrest for incest and both were charged with performing the abortion.

On March 20, 1950, DA investigators Lt. Jemison and Walter Morgan interview Charles Smith's girlfriend, Mildred Bray and discover she witnessed a $1,000 cash payoff from Hodel to Smith. The payoff was made on December 29, 1949, just four days after Hodel's "acquittal" on the child molestation charges. Smith implicated and identified by Tamar is quoted in Lt. Jemison's report as saying:

"Someday I'm going to fix Tamar. I'm going to cut a chunk out of the calf of her leg and fry it and eat it in front of her eyes and then puke it up in front of her face."

On this very first day of recorded conversations we have George Hodel admitting to the murder of Elizabeth Short, payoffs to law enforcement and bragging about his influence in having officers demoted and transferred in connection with his incest trial.

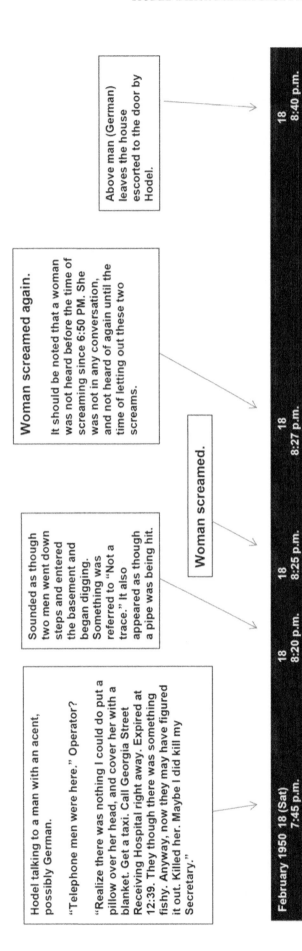

Above man (German) leaves the house escorted to the door by Hodel.

Woman screamed again.

It should be noted that a woman was not heard before the time of screaming since 6:50 PM. She was not in any conversation, and not heard of again until the time of letting out these two screams.

Woman screamed.

Hodel talking to a man with an acent, possibly German.

"Telephone men were here." Operator?

"Realize there was nothing I could do put a pillow over her head, and cover her with a blanket. Get a taxi. Call Georgia Street Receiving Hospital right away. Expired at 12:39. They though there was something fishy. Anyway, now they may have figured it out. Killed her. Maybe I did kill my Secretary."

Sounded as though two men went down steps and entered the basement and began digging. Something was referred to "Not a trace." It also appeared as though a pipe was being hit.

February 1950 18 (Sat)
7:45 p.m.
Crowley LAPD
Arrives records above

18
8:20 p.m.

18
8:25 p.m.

18
8:27 p.m.

18
8:40 p.m.

AUTHOR NOTES

[Boxed statements are verbatim as they appear on original transcripts including spelling errors]

Of the forty-days of George Hodel recorded conversations, these words, heard on Feb. 18 are unquestionably the most ominous. What the officers are here recording could well have been an actual "murder in progress." Our time-line three hours earlier established that an unidentified woman was crying and made several attempts to call the Telephone Operator. Nothing more is heard from her until the beating sounds in the basement followed by two screams from her just minutes apart. Digging sounds are heard and an admonishment to "not leave a trace." [Note- In 1950 the basement in our Franklin Home was earth, not cement.] Nothing further is heard from the woman. No mention of her ever leaving the house. Speaking as a trained police officer, it is incomprehensible to me why the detectives [Crowley LAPD & McGrath DA] TOOK NO ACTION? The location was 5 minutes away from their listening post at Hollywood Station. At the very least they were monitoring a serious felony assault and based on what we hear on these transcripts, it was more likely - an actual MURDER. The correct police response here would have been to attempt an immediate rescue of this victim by rushing to the Hodel residence and kicking in the door. Some will counter that, "Well, they didn't want to blow their cover and their case." My response, - Consider the fact that they already had his confession to two separate murders- ON TAPE.

Dr. Hodel's earlier, 7:45 p.m. admissions to the German [Now known and identified as Baron Ernst von Harringa] relate to the 1945 overdose murder of Dr. Hodel's First Street V.D. clinic secretary, Ruth Spaulding. My follow-up investigation into her death showed that she was brought to Georgia Street Receiving Hospital by cab on May 10, 1945 and pronounced dead at approximately 12:39 a.m. Spaulding likely knew that George Hodel was seeing and possibly medically treating Elizabeth Short and was the "unidentified doctor" referenced in the DA reports. Ruth could and certainly would have provided detectives this information eighteen months later, had she still been alive. [Hence the relevance of George Hodel's admission on tape, "Supposin' I did kill the Black Dahlia, they can't prove it anymore, because my secretary is dead."]

6

(Hodel/Kenneth Rexroth continuing conversation)

Hodel: "I'm selling my art collection Monday and Tuesday, and I'm then taking off for Asia.

Rexroth: "I am in process of breaking up with my wife of 15 years. No children."

Hodel: "I have 3 boys. You'll see them later. Dorothy lives here a while, and then takes off."

Rexroth: "What about M?"

Hodel: "She is on staff of San Francisco Chronicle. Art Editor, had a serious operation.

Conversation with a patient.

...

Talking with a man about some special treatment apparently syphilis and marital troubles....The man leaves with instructions to call Wednesday.

Lady talking in distance. (sounds like maid's voice) It sounded as though she said, "are there any more cops around." Heard no answer.

Hodel & Ellen enter room. Hodel—"Will you leave the light on there. I'm just a little nervous. Hodel say's he is worried. Ellen admires a Chinese box. Hodel say's a Manchurian princess gave it to him. He say's he is going to sell it.

Ellen wants to stay with him, he tells her to go to bed, she can stay with him tomorrow. Movements around the room. Low conversation, unable to make out. Deep breathing. Hodel and Ellen probably having intercourse...Definite sounds of climax of intercourse. Hodel sighs loudly and passionately.

February 1950 19
12:00 p.m.
Jemison DA

19
3:00 p.m.

19
4:54 p.m.
(Hronek on duty)

20
9:10 p.m.
(Crowley LAPD relieves Walter Morgan)

22
2:10 a.m.
(Brechel LAPD on duty)

22
2:45 a.m.

AUTHOR NOTES

[Boxed statements are verbatim as they appear on original transcripts including spelling errors]

Kenneth Rexroth was a well-known writer and poet from the San Francisco Bay area. Many consider him to be "the Father of the Beat Generation." He was a friend of both my parents, George and Dorero Hodel as well as other Franklin house guests such as surreal artist Man Ray and his wife, Juliet and writer Henry Miller.

I believe Rexroth's question as to "M" refers to EMILIA, George Hodel's ex-wife, and the mother of my older half-brother, Duncan Hodel. Emilia was then living in San Francisco. Thirty-seven years later, in 1987, Emilia, still living in the S.F. Bay area, would take her own life by ingesting an overdose of barbiturates.

Timeline:

February 1950 22	24	24	26	26	26
12:35 p.m.	1:20 p.m.	4:25 p.m.	9:30 p.m.	9:50 p.m.	10:30 p.m.
Morgan DA's office On duty (spool 10)	Sullivan DA on duty (spool 14)	Hronek DA on duty	Crowley LAPD on duty (spool 19)		

Telephone rang—Hodel—"Oh yeah Power- are you in town-good-things are sort of busy right now for the next ten days-we're tapped now again-well there is pretty much going on regarding yourself and me. I was questioned about you and so forth- maybe you can find out- Don't you know someone up there? Maybe you can find out what the hell is going on up there. I would like to see you in person when we get a chance- what's your phone? That's your new phone? (Ends) "OK- so long.""

(Hodel) Dials phone (recorded) asks for new car salesman..."I've got a 1936 Packard Sedan to trade in. Want to make Packard down payment."

Phone rings. Hodel answered- Ellen took over- still talking about the citizenship. Hodel, "Ellen didn't I tell you not to tell people things over the telephone....Ellen said something about the FBI investigating us.

(Hodel conversation with man & woman) Hodel wisecracks— Hodel—"a peculiar people, the Persians, the country produces no virgins. They fuck all day in a violent way, and at night they practice sexual perversions."

(Hodel) Talking about insuring something value $76,000. "If you want to sell it you would get $750." Trinkets. Hodel had it insured for $104,000. Alimony payments $300 month. Getting it reduced.

Hodel mentions something about MURDER.

Los Angeles Times
July 14, 1949

Deputy to Conduct Finance Inquiry

Dist. Atty. William E. Simpson yesterday placed Dep. Dist. Att. Joseph Power in charge of the Guarantee Finance Co. investigation.

Nearly 40 witnesses are to be interviewed to learn whether there is basis for prosecution. The Governor's Crime Commission has charged the company is a "front" for a $7,000,000 bookmaking syndicate which has paid $247,000 in bribes to Southland law enforcement officers last year.

Tom Doherty, District Attorney's auditor, and State Public Utilities Commission's auditors have been studying the company's books for two weeks.

DDA Joseph Power
Assigned 1949

CHINESE TABLET VALUED AT $25,000 TAKEN BY BURGLAR

A 1400-year-old Chinese sacrificial tablet, valued at $25,000, was stolen early yesterday from the home of Dr. George H. Hodel, 5121 Franklin Ave., according to police.

The burglar entered the home through a rear bedroom window. Dr. Hodel described the antique as 11 by 6 by 3½ inches, bearing about 50 Chinese characters carved on a dark gray stone.

Los Angeles Times
Nov. 20, 1947

"...has charged the company [GFC] is a "front" for a $7,000,000 bookmaking syndicate which paid $247,000 in bribes to Southland law enforcement officers last year."

AUTHOR NOTES

[Boxed statements are verbatim as they appear on original transcript with spelling errors]

George Hodel's conversation with "Power" could *possibly* be Dep. District Attorney, Joseph Power, then an active DA involved in the prosecution of a major booking making operation with payoffs to corrupt cops. [Guarantee Finance Company] DDA Power at this time was seven-months into the case and actively preparing for trial which would begin in March, 1950.

On this tape he tells "Power" that "they [DA investigators] are checking out connections between "you and me." On an earlier tape we have George Hodel saying, "This is the best payoff I've seen between law enforcement agencies." The Guarantee Finance scandal was one of the largest bookmaking operations in the 1940s with payoffs ("juice") to law enforcement agencies estimated by the Kefauver Commission to be approximate $212,000 per year.

The 10:30 p.m. entry re. "trinkets" is interesting in light of the fact that George Hodel on 11.20.47 reported a valuable "1400-year-old Chinese sacrificial tablet was taken from the Franklin House in "a burglary." He claimed it was worth $25,000. In post war U.S. dollars he may have purchased it in China as a "reproduction" for as little as $50.00. In the conversation he admits the insurance scam or another just like it. [See *L.A. Times* articles on George Hodel's Franklin House "burglary" and DDA Power's appointment to head GFC prosecution at right.]

February 1950 27 12:00 a.m.	27 12:25 a.m. (spool 21)	27 12:35 a.m.	27 12:50 a.m.	27 1:14 a.m.

Door bell rings. Ellen goes to door. Hodel, "You made headlines today or tomorrow." Man- "Headlines? Hodel- "Like Hitler said, Your a rich man. I can see you beating her up."

... Man (laughing) "Suspicion." Hah. In one place I am a composer of poetry or opera, a hot tempered erratic woman- We've got to get out of here and get some fun for a change."

Hodel- "Well anyway she hasn't said she'd committed incest or killed the Black Dahlia. (other man has an accent, talking about this country.) Man- "She said look what you've put in the paper. I hate you."

Hodel- "It wouldn't do any harm to wait another month. There are other type of penicillin who are more apt to get the rash on the second—"

(Juvenile officers observed a 41 cream 4 door Buick parked in front of Hodel's residence at this time. License #751014 registered to Etoyle E. Bennett- Legal owner, Hollywood Citizen News.)

Hodel- "We'll really have to ride herd on them. 4 young chicks in a strange country.

Man- "Ha- 4 young girls and we two- what a combination." ...

Hodel- "I'm the only person who knows where all these things fit into the picture."

Hodel- "You better take a generous supply of penicillin. (Talking to same party)

AUTHOR NOTES

[Boxed statements are verbatim as they appear on original transcripts including spelling errors]

The man talking to Hodel is identified as Theodore Kolline, a "composer, poet and painter." As Hodel indicates on the wire, the article did appear in the newspapers later in the day. The vehicle parked outside may have been borrowed and driven by Kolline, but showed registered to the Hollywood Citizen News, one of L.A.'s six newspapers.

On this surveillance tape we hear George Hodel making more references to the Black Dahlia murder and to his committing incest. Most interesting is his reference that, "HE ALONE KNOWS WHERE ALL THESE THINGS FIT INTO THE PICTURE."

See *L.A. Times* article on Composer Kolline dated Feb. 27, on right.

L.A. Times Feb. 27, 1950

Composer Kolline and Protege Feud in Explosive Divorce Suit

"Two explosive complaints for divorce are all that remain from the romance which began when Theodore Kolline, 46, orchestra conductor, composer, poet and painter, made Mrs. Renee Kolline, 22, his artistic protégé.

The two suits were filed almost simultaneously in Superior Court. Mrs. Kolline presented the first petition, charging that her husband mistreated her during the four months they lived together.

When they first met, she told the court, Kolline became her teacher and later induced her to marry him. They were wed in Santa Ana last Oct. 13. Immediately thereafter, Mrs. Kolline says, her husband undertook to train her as a classical dancer, vocalist and agreed to maintain her in a style in keeping with his position in the world of art.

Seeks Alimony

Mrs. Kolline complains that cruel treatment on his part forced her to part from him last Feb. 21. She asks that he be compelled to pay her alimony commensurate with the style in which she contends he promised to maintain her when they were wed.

Kolline's own suit also charges cruelty and asserts that his young wife made off with unmounted jade worth $500, his account books and other documents representing $2900 he held in trust as president of the Beethoven Society of America. He demands return of the property. Mrs. Kolline sued through Attys. C. Paul Dubois and Edward Cotter and her husband through Atty. Victor Ford Collins.

9

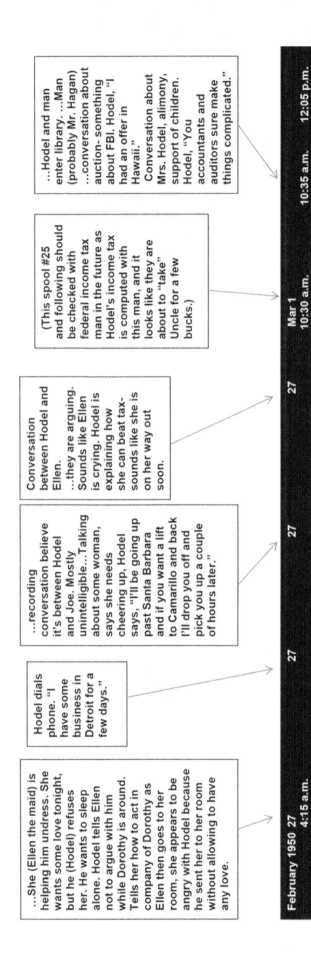

...She (Ellen the maid) is helping him undress. She wants some love tonight, but he (Hodel) refuses her. He wants to sleep alone. Hodel tells Ellen not to argue with him while Dorothy is around. Tells her how to act in company of Dorothy as Ellen then goes to her room, she appears to be angry with Hodel because he sent her to her room without allowing to have any love.

Hodel dials phone. "I have some business in Detroit for a few days."

...recording conversation believe it's between Hodel and Joe. Mostly unintelligible...Talking about some woman, says she needs cheering up, Hodel says, "I'll be going up past Santa Barbara and if you want a lift to Camarillo and back I'll drop you off and pick you up a couple of hours later."

Conversation between Hodel and Ellen. ...they are arguing. Sounds like Ellen is crying. Hodel is explaining how she can beat tax- sounds like she is on her way out soon.

(This spool #25 and following should be checked with federal income tax man in the future as Hodel's income tax is computed with this man, and it looks like they are about to "take" Uncle for a few bucks.)

...Hodel and man enter library. ...Man (probably Mr. Hagan) ...conversation about auction- something about FBI. Hodel, "I had an offer in Hawaii." Conversation about Mrs. Hodel, alimony, support of children. Hodel, "You accountants and auditors sure make things complicated."

Hodel still in conversation with his acct. (being recorded) (Spools 25 & 26 and 27 will prove very interesting to income tax investigators.)

February 1950 27	27	27	Mar 1		
4:15 a.m.	2:05p.m.	8:45 p.m.	11:10 p.m.	10:30 a.m.	10:35 a.m. 12:05 p.m.
Brechel, LAPD On duty (spool 22)				Morgan DA office on duty (spool 25)	

AUTHOR NOTES

[Boxed statements are verbatim as they appear on original transcripts including spelling errors]

Above reference to woman at Camarillo refers to Lillian Lenorak, the witness who admitted to committing perjury at George Hodel's incest trial and then later at Dr. Leslie C. Ballard and Charles Smith's trial for performing Tamar abortion. Lillian Lenorak, Officer Mary Unkefer story summarized in previous chapter of this book.

| March 1950 | 1 11:37 p.m. Meyer, LAPD | 3 4:10 a.m. Brechel LAPD (spool 21) | 3 12:07 p.m. Sullivan DA | 3 1:11 p.m. | 4 1:21 p.m. | 4 2:45 p.m. | 4 3:26 p.m. |

Phone rang. Hodel answered. Whoever he was talking to he said, "Don't say anything over the phone- it is tapped- said he had there phone number, and would call tomorrow-said he would have to go out to call-said if he said phone number, "They" would be out and bother them- that is what "They" always do. When Hodel hung up, Ellen asked him how he knew- Hodel said he was just talking.

Hodel and Ellen have conversation is Spanish. They are in bedroom having sex intercourse or something, probably perversion. Sounds like he got another blow job.

...Conversation between Hodel and Woman. Woman, "I owe 4 times 75.00, that's 300.00 (possibly his wife) "I have to pay my rent or get out." Conversation with woman continues. Relative to her expenses and the childrens. ...Conversation with wife resumed. Hodel, "I've lost money every year." Talking about what money she's earned. Hodel discusses his lossess of that year. Now I must sell the house. Hodel, something about pennitentirary. Noises in background.

Conversation with woman. (wife) She's talking about the children. Hodel talks about having wife and children with him again.

Phone rings. Hodel answers (recorded) "Your'e talking over a tapped line. Oh yes, it's been tapped for a long time. I'll be home for the next hour. Be sure and come.

Man still talking – (recorded) talking to Hodel about some woman. Mentions Barbara Sherman, Dorothy Black (?) Something about Santa Barbara. Hodel- "She called me this morning. She's coming over this P.M." Man- "You had pretty good success with some of those dames I fixed."

Hodel to man, "In about 2 or 3 weeks I'll probably be on way abroad."

L.A. Times Feb. 1, 1950

Probation Given in Morals Case

Barbara Sherman given probation ordered not to see/associate with Dr. Hodel.

AUTHOR NOTES

[Boxed statements are verbatim as they appear on original transcripts including spelling errors]

Based on above response it is obvious George Hodel was just guessing that his phone was "tapped." When maid, Ellen, asks him "how he knows?" he responds by saying, "he is just talking." Hodel's reference to "they" obviously refers to, LAPD & DA detectives. Clearly, he has no suspicion that the rooms have concealed microphones and are "wired for sound."

Barbara Sherman [Shearman] was a star witness in the 1949 incest trial and present in the bedroom when Hodel & Sexton had the sex acts with George's 14-year-old daughter, Tamar. Shearman testified at the preliminary hearing to being present and seeing the sex acts. She then refused to testify at the later Superior Court trial and was arrested for perjury, based on her previous sworn testimony. On Feb. 1, 1950, she was allowed to plead guilty to a lesser charge [Contributing to a Minor] and as the L.A. Times article indicates, was given straight probation.

What is of particular interest here is the conversation between Hodel and the unidentified male caller on March 4th. The conversation centers on Barbara Sherman and despite the judge's order to "keep away" Hodel tells the man that "she is coming over this PM." [Sounds like he is talking about Sherman?] Then the man reminds Hodel that he had "good success with some of those dames I fixed." One has to wonder based on the earlier conversation if the "fixed" refers to their witness testimony? [The DA Files mention a $15,000 payoff-bribe paid by Hodel through his attorney to secure an acquittal.]

George Hodel, true to his word, leaves later that month [March 28] leaving the surveillance teams "staked out" on an empty house.

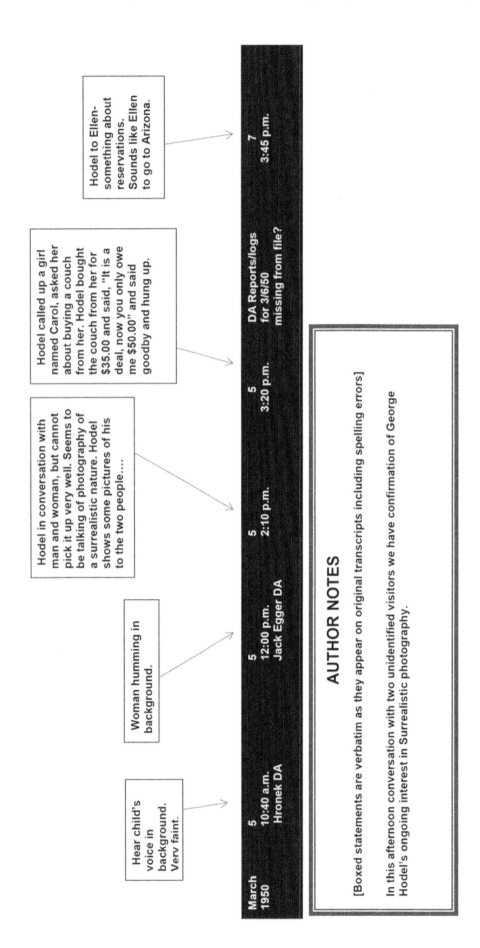

Hear child's voice in background. Very faint.

Woman humming in background.

Hodel in conversation with man and woman, but cannot pick it up very well. Seems to be talking of photography of a surrealistic nature. Hodel shows some pictures of his to the two people....

Hodel called up a girl named Carol, asked her about buying a couch from her. Hodel bought the couch from her for $35.00 and said, "It is a deal, now you only owe me $50.00" and said goodby and hung up.

Hodel to Ellen- something about reservations. Sounds like Ellen to go to Arizona.

March 1950

5
10:40 a.m.
Hronek DA

5
12:00 p.m.
Jack Egger DA

5
2:10 p.m.

5
3:20 p.m.

7
3:45 p.m.

DA Reports/logs for 3/6/50 missing from file?

AUTHOR NOTES

[Boxed statements are verbatim as they appear on original transcripts including spelling errors]

In this afternoon conversation with two unidentified visitors we have confirmation of George Hodel's ongoing interest in Surrealistic photography.

March 1950	8 10:30 a.m. McGrath DA	8 8:10 p.m. Meyer LAPD	9 9:50 a.m. Brechel LAPD	9 10:00 a.m.	9 10:55 a.m.	10 12:15 a.m.

Conversation over phone with his wife Dorothy- she was complaining about money- he said "he is broke- can't pay mortgage on the house this month- has no money coming in" from sounds of conversation bad feelings may be developing.

Hodel phones someone and asks name and exact title of Chief of States of Burma and Tibet- wants to know how they are addressed. Name of Minister Public Health of Burma. Goes back to typing.

Hodel talking with man with German accent- talking about going to the auction and buying and selling things…

Hodel phones Telephone Company to have extension of OL 3476 disconnected.

Officer Bimson and Sgt. Belle checked Hodel's residence for license plates to find out who man with German accent is- the following plates were in sun in front of Hodel's house.
35 Packard F.E. Mattoon….
47 Chev. Willie Wheeler…
41 Ford Violet Jean Wallen…
36 Packard Marie L. Valla…..

One or two men and about same amount of women— talking to Hodel. Hard to understand—something about a place in Mexico not too far from AZ—good roads—something about a Whore House, or sanatarium. One man seems to be a doctor. Talking about she at Camarillo. Hodel- "She was going to shoot me and commit suicide- "Tamara" (way it sounded) Talking about fishing trip to Mexico …looking at map—mentioned Sonora, Mexico. …says he will leave - Hodel know about noon tomorrow-Friday about trip.

AUTHOR NOTES

[Boxed statements are verbatim as they appear on original transcripts including spelling errors]

The March 10 "she – Camarillo" entry refers to Lillian Lenorak and is independent corroboration to statements made by witness/roomer, Joe Barrett who came home to the Franklin House in Jan. 1950, to find Lenorak in George Hodel's bedroom holding his loaded rifle and threatening to kill George "for what he had done." Barrett in a 2003 on-camera television interview stated that this referred to the murder of Elizabeth Short. Barrett claims he took the rifle away from Lenorak "and calmed her down." This incident and the fact that Lenorak threatened George Hodel that "she was going to tell the DA that she had committed perjury in both Dr. Hodel and Dr. Ballard's trials" likely was what precipitated the drugging and superficial cutting of her wrists BY DR. HODEL. This staged "attempt suicide" by Hodel as documented in the officer Mary Unkefer/Lenorak Letter, was his way of discrediting Lenorak and getting her admitted to Camarillo hospital for temporary observation for being "emotionally distraught." This March 10 conversation occurred about ten days after officer Unkefer picked up Lenorak from the Franklin House and transported her to Santa Barbara and then wrote her letter to the DA informing them of Dr. Hodel's actions.

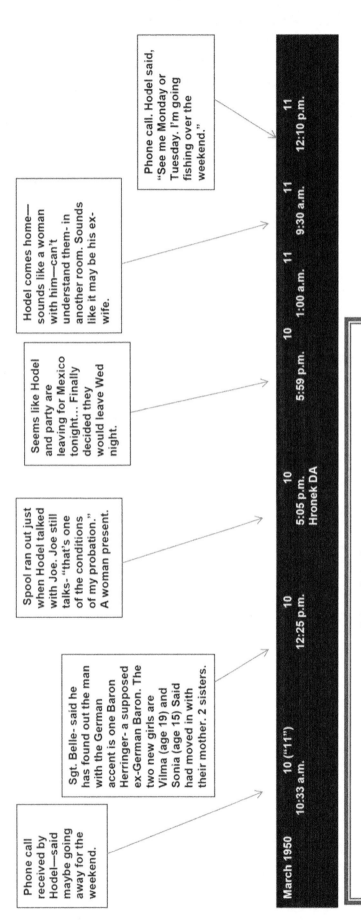

Phone call received by Hodel—said maybe going away for the weekend.

Sgt. Belle- said he has found out the man with the German accent is one Baron Herringer- a supposed ex-German Baron. The two new girls are Vilma (age 19) and Sonia (age 15) Said had moved in with their mother. 2 sisters.

Spool ran out just when Hodel talked with Joe. Joe still talks- "that's one of the conditions of my probation." A woman present.

Seems like Hodel and party are leaving for Mexico tonight…. Finally decided they would leave Wed night.

Hodel comes home—sounds like a woman with him—can't understand them- in another room. Sounds like it may be his ex-wife.

Phone call. Hodel said, "See me Monday or Tuesday. I'm going fishing over the weekend."

March 1950	10 ("11")	10	10	10	11	11	11	11
	10:33 a.m.	12:25 p.m.	5:05 p.m. Hronek DA	5:59 p.m.	1:00 a.m.	9:30 a.m.	12:10 p.m.	

AUTHOR NOTES

[Boxed statements are verbatim as they appear on original transcripts including spelling errors]

Appears officers misdated above as "11", actually MAR 10.

Officers misspelled name as "Baron Herringer," which prevented further identification. As summarized in an earlier chapter, I was able to positively identify "The Baron" as, Ernst von Harringa, an art dealer, and close friend of George Hodel's, as well as his probable accomplice to a felony assault and or murder as recorded on earlier taped transcripts of Feb. 18. [See following chapter, "The Baron" for complete details.]

In the 5:05 p.m. entry Joe Barrett informs his landlord, George Hodel about "the conditions of his probation." Barrett was placed on probation related to "Contributing to a Minor" related to his involvement with Tamar, some six months prior, in the summer of 1949. We also know that at this time the DA investigators were using Joe Barrett as "their mole" inside the Franklin House.

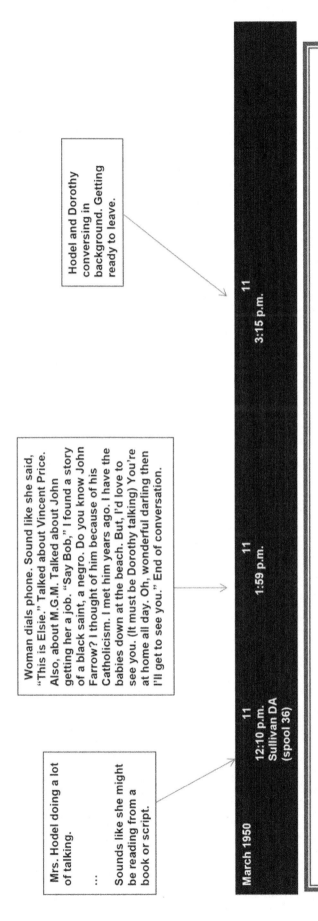

Mrs. Hodel doing a lot of talking.

…

Sounds like she might be reading from a book or script.

Woman dials phone. Sound like she said, "This is Elsie." Talked about Vincent Price. Also, about M.G.M. Talked about John getting her a job. "Say Bob," I found a story of a black saint, a negro. Do you know John Farrow? I thought of him because of his Catholicism. I met him years ago. But, I'd love to see you. (It must be Dorothy talking) You're at home all day. Oh, wonderful darling then I'll get to see you." End of conversation.

Hodel and Dorothy conversing in background. Getting ready to leave.

| March 1950 | 11 12:10 p.m. Sullivan DA (spool 36) | 11 1:59 p.m. | 11 3:15 p.m. |

AUTHOR NOTES

[Boxed statements are verbatim as they appear on original transcripts including spelling errors]

Dorothy Hodel previously wrote scripts for MGM, RKO, and other Hollywood studios. "John" is her ex-husband, John Huston, whom she did rewrites for as recently as 1947. (*Treasure of the Sierra Madre*) It is significant that she mentions film director John Farrow. Farrow is relevant to the investigation for the following reasons:

In the early 1940s, film director, John Farrow, then married to actress Maureen O'Sullivan, had an affair with Lillian Lenorak, then a young dancer with the famed Ruth St. Denis studio. A son, John was born out of this relationship, and was the three-year-old child, who witnessed the assault on his mother by George Hodel at the Franklin House in January, 1950. ["He hit mommie hard and hurt her."] John Lenorak in adulthood changed his name to Farrow and is the half-brother of Mia Farrow. John Farrow Jr. died in 2010.

Tragically, John Lenorak's mother, Lillian, was murdered near Palm Springs in 1959. The crime was a random act committed by a disturbed 21-year-old who was arrested a week later. The Lenorak murder WAS NOT RELATED OR CONNECTED IN ANY WAY TO GEORGE HODEL.

Three months after this police surveillance ended, Director John Farrow released a film-noir [made in 1949] *WHERE DANGER LIVES.* The story involves: a woman who attempts suicide, a young doctor who falls in love with her, a murder, and their fleeing to Mexico. Cast in a bit part in the film was an attractive Eurasian actress, Kiyo Cuddy, the ex-lover of George Hodel and the future wife to be [1962] of Steve Hodel.

Hodel answered over the phone about his fishing in Mexico and dropping Ellen off in some town. Hoping she won't have enough money to return. (recorded)

Hodel on phone- "I just got back yesterday- It's 65 miles across the border from Arizona- Sonita (?) Fishing good. Talked to Dr. Ignacia Renal (?) much interested in making a sanitorium out of the place.

...

Another Dr. and associates of mine went down there today to look at it. Would clear about 5000.00 month. When you come in from Upland the next time, bring her with you so I can meet. Upland 024277 is her phone number. She is a nurse.

Hodel dials phone "Is Mr. Ed Wilcox there." "Something about Ed being able to receive a message from Tibet. "I'm expecting a message from Mr.? of Tibet." (Ed is apparently a ham short-waver)

Woman leave- Hodel and man with accent-talking recorded- hard to hear. Hodel say's probably they are watching me, talks about selling some of his stuff at an auction-says someone don't know anything to tell. Hodel said something about getting married again-talks about place in Mexico. Says it will clear about 4 or 5,000 a month...

Hodel—"Do you think those "Bastards" will try to bring action because I am renting rooms." Hodel says "Do you think we could hire some girl to find out what they are doing."

...

Man with accent left.

March 1950	14 4:13 p.m. Hronek DA	15 1:06 p.m.	15 3:15 p.m.	17 11:30 p.m.	18 12:40 a.m.

AUTHOR NOTES

[Boxed statements are verbatim as they appear on original transcripts including spelling errors]

George Hodel looking into setting up what sounds like an abortion clinic just across the border, which he estimates could pull in 4-5K a month which in 1950 dollars would have been equivalent to about $50,000. On the 1:06 p.m. entry he mentions that a local doctor and "associates" went with him to Mexico to check out the potentials of the clinic. On other taped discussion he mentions that the clinic, being across the border in Sonora, would "be safe."

Man with "accent" is probably Baron Harringa since George is talking to him about selling art works. Also, mentions trying to get girls to obtain information from "those Bastards" which is obviously City authorities.

16

A woman comes to see Hodel—sounds like Dorothy—they go to rear of house can't hear.

Hodel and Dorothy engage in a little loving.

Hodel phones someone about $50.00 a month he paid some woman. Said "I'm in trouble" want some advice- do you have a farm.

Hodel and some guy with accent talking and looking at map of Mexico. (The photographer) ...Talking about going (to Mexico) want to leave tomorrow night, Hodel says don't tell anyone. Hodel says he has to be back Wed. He is going to Santa Barbara, and won't be back until Sunday. Sounds like they are going to take pictures. Sounds like Hodel is trying to pull a fast one of some kind.

Phone call received- can't hear- too much racket- Hodel has dinner engagement tonight. Going out of town Wed. Hodel talking about selling the house.

Hodel answers door bell, lets in woman- he talks to her about renting her a room in return he will knock off the rent- an work she does for him such as cleaning and taking care of his quarters. Phone rings- Hodel says "Mrs. Hodel is out- I can take message. He said he is going down to the beach about 4pm today- talks about renting room. Hodel again talking to Negro woman. Woman starts talking about doctors- Hodel tells her about his clinic at 1st & Central. Woman said she had a curetement (?) in 1944. Hodel said he has done lots of them. Hodel and woman continue to talk about doctors, sickness and other medical subjects. (Hodel seems to be acting overly nice to this woman. He must be trying to talk her into renting the room, or?) Hodel tells her that Dr. Hill, a colored doctor, lives next door. ....Woman leaves.

March 1950					
19	20	20	21	21	21
1:45 p.m.	10:15 a.m.	10:50 p.m.	10:55 a.m.	11:05 a.m.	1:00 p.m.
Egger DA (spool 37)	McGrath DA	Meyer LAPD	McGrath DA	McGrath DA	

AUTHOR NOTES

[Boxed statements are verbatim as they appear on original transcripts including spelling errors]

Here we have Dr. Hodel actually admitting on tape that he has performed many surgical abortions! "I've done lots of them." The term currettement is synonymous with what is known as a "D&C"- Dilation & Curettage. Here is the medical definition:

"A gynecological procedure performed on the female reproductive system that used to be a common method of abortion. The procedure involves dilating the cervix and inserting instruments to clean out the lining of the uterus, which can include an embryo or fetus, while the woman is under an anesthetic. Curettage is performed with a curette, a metal rod with a handle on one end and a sharp loop on the other."

Dr. Charles Hill, a dentist and our neighbor directly to the west of the Franklin House, was a highly respected member of L.A.'s Black Community and reportedly a "Mover & Shaker" in 1940s local politics. Joe Barrett mentions Dr. Hill owned a bail bonds company and was the one who put up the bail on Barrett's "Contributing" arrest. The following day, after bailing Joe out of jail, Dr. Hill invited him to accompany him to a swank gathering where Joe recalls the mayor, police chief and other City officials were in attendance.

The March 21 1:00 p.m. entry underscores that despite my parent's five-year divorce, they still remain on *intimate* terms.

DA investigator Jack Egger appears on a number of stake-outs throughout the surveillance. Egger after leaving the DA's Office will join Beverly Hills Police Department and promote to Captain of Detectives. He will then become Chief of Security at Warner Brothers Studio. In a strange coincidence, this same Jack Egger in 1946-7 was a young head-usher at *Columbia Broadcasting Studios* in Hollywood, and was familiar with Elizabeth Short on sight as she regularly attended the radio shows. In a later chapter of this book I detail the connections between Egger and Short and his 2003 positive identification of Dr. George Hodel as being the man with her at CBS studios, just days before her murder.

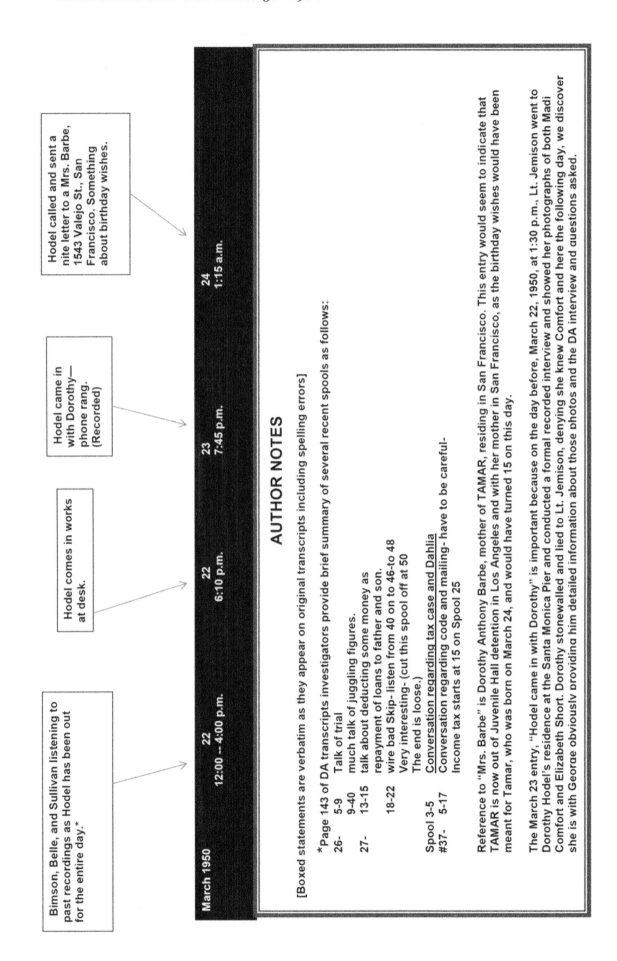

Bimson, Belle, and Sullivan listening to past recordings as Hodel has been out for the entire day.*

Hodel comes in works at desk.

Hodel came in with Dorothy— phone rang. (Recorded)

Hodel called and sent a nite letter to a Mrs. Barbe, 1543 Valejo St., San Francisco. Something about birthday wishes.

March 1950

22	22	23	24
12:00 – 4:00 p.m.	6:10 p.m.	7:45 p.m.	1:15 a.m.

AUTHOR NOTES

[Boxed statements are verbatim as they appear on original transcripts including spelling errors]

*Page 143 of DA transcripts investigators provide brief summary of several recent spools as follows:

26- 5-9   Talk of trial
9-40   much talk of juggling figures.
27- 13-15   talk about deducting some money as
repayment of loans to father and son.
18-22   wire bad Skip- listen from 40 on to 46-to 48
Very interesting- (cut this spool off at 50
The end is loose.)
Spool 3-5   Conversation regarding tax case and Dahlia
#37- 5-17   Conversation regarding code and mailing- have to be careful-
Income tax starts at 15 on Spool 25

Reference to "Mrs. Barbe" is Dorothy Anthony Barbe, mother of TAMAR, residing in San Francisco. This entry would seem to indicate that TAMAR is now out of Juvenile Hall detention in Los Angeles and with her mother in San Francisco, as the birthday wishes would have been meant for Tamar, who was born on March 24, and would have turned 15 on this day.

The March 23 entry, "Hodel came in with Dorothy" is important because on the day before, March 22, 1950, at 1:30 p.m., Lt. Jemison went to Dorothy Hodel's residence at the Santa Monica Pier and conducted a formal recorded interview and showed her photographs of both Madi Comfort and Elizabeth Short. Dorothy stonewalled and lied to Lt. Jemison, denying she knew Comfort and here the following day, we discover she is with George obviously providing him detailed information about those photos and the DA interview and questions asked.

March 1950	25 11:10 p.m. Meyer, LAPD	26 12:00 a.m. (spool 39)	26 1:00 a.m. (spool 40)	26 8:00 p.m. Meyer LAPD (spool 41)	26 11:55 p.m.	27 2:00 a.m.

[Box — 25, 11:10 p.m.]

Hodel and Baron (man with accent) came in talking low—can't hear (recording) only stays few minutes and leaves. I was wrong—in bathroom. Sounded like Hodel said something about Black Daliah. Baron said something about FBI Then talked about Tibet- sound like Hodel wants to get out of the country—mentioned passport—Hodel giving Baron dope on how to write to Tibet. Hodel talking about Mexico—going down and take pictures and write a story. Hodel seems afraid about something. Hodel says his Sanatarium—if he got is started in Mexico—would be "Safe."

[Box — spool 39/40]

Spool ran out—changing—talking about woman. …Hodel says he wants money and power—talking about Chine—talking about selling some of Hodel's paintings or something. Hodel talking about picture police have of him and some girl—thought he had destroyed them all—wire quit at 50—new one going on—not much talk.

[Box — 8:00 p.m. / 11:55 p.m.]

Had trouble with one spool. Had to use another—still talking about selling paintings.

…

Sounds like Baron left—don't know if there is anything on these records or not.

[Box — 11:55 p.m.]

Hodel- some woman come in also the Baron. Hodel and Baron talking low.

[Box — 27, 2:00 a.m.]

All quiet. Good nite.

AUTHOR NOTES

[Boxed statements are verbatim as they appear on original transcripts including spelling errors]

THE DA/LAPD SURVEILLANCE-STAKE-OUT UNEXPECTEDLY ENDS HERE, WITH GEORGE HODEL EITHER BEING TIPPED OFF OR DECIDING ON HIS OWN THAT THINGS ARE TOO HOT.

He splits, literally leaving the DA/LAPD teams with their microphones in the walls of the Franklin House.

On this last night we hear Hodel confiding to his accomplice, Baron Harringa of, "wanting to get out of the country", the "FBI", talking about "The Black Dahlia," and "pictures police have of him and a girl" which Hodel says, he "thought he had destroyed."

Just four days earlier, on March 22, 1950 DA Lt. Frank Jemison interviewed Dorothy Hodel at her home on Santa Monica Pier *and informed her that Elizabeth "Black Dahlia" Short had been identified by witnesses as "knowing and being with Dr. Hodel at the Franklin House before the murder."* Lt. Jemison further confronts Dorothy with the fact that he had information that she had stated to Tamar Hodel that George Hodel, a day or two after the crime, came home intoxicated and said, "They will never be able to pin that murder on me." [In his closing typed report, Jemison presents the actual wording as, "They will never be able to prove I did that murder." In her interview, Dorothy stonewalls Lt. Jemison, denying any knowledge, and lying about not knowing Madi (Mattie) Comfort. [As we now know, George and Dorothy and Madi were lovers in the 1940s] Then on the following day, we discover she meets and provides George with the details of the interview and the fact the police have the photographs.

While it sounds like George Hodel may have initially taken off for Mexico, we cannot be sure, where he went and how long he was absent. New details will be presented in a later chapter providing updated information on this subject.

19

Original Unabridged
Hodel-Black Dahlia D.A. Transcripts

HODEL FILE

FEBURRY 18, 1950   10:00AM

SPOOL #1 Intermittant recordings while set was being installed.

BIMSON

Spool
Time

0-3½	10:05A	Hodel talking to Ellen about Lawyer.
3½-5	10:15A	Talking to Ellen about marrying susie.
-5½		Unable to understand.
	10:20A	Telephoning - unable to hear conversation.

BROWNSON

	10:45A	7 minutes - telephone conversation pertaining to medical work
	11:00A	11 minutes - telephone call Dr. Hodel makes appointment for 3:00 to 4:00 PM with Mr. Betty? Conversation with housekeeper.
	11:45A	Trouble developed on phone line. Slop over - mostly did clicks - some occasional cross talk. Occasional dial tone. Trouble developed suddenly. Mikes still hot. Recording made at 24 minutes.
	12:10P	Tone line cleared.

LYLEY
FRANK HRONEK
February 18, 1950 12:00 noon

Spool #1 Log

	12:31	Moving around the house.
	12:36	Phone rang - answered - conversation at 5:30 PM-see someone
	12:39	End of conversation.
	12:54	Very bad reception
	12:56	Moving around the house.
	12:59	Typing

HODEL FILE

February 13, 1950
Spool #1 Log

2

Spool
Time

	1:07	Calling someone - hello this is George Hodel.
	1:09	End of conversation
	1:11	Typing
	1:13	Typine stopped - just moving around
	1:18	Dialing - asking for at 66403 HI 3477 VA 9060
		Traying various numbers.
	1:32	End of conversation - calling someone else - Betty
	1:35	End of conversation
	1:38	Moving around
	1:43	Received call
	1:45	Made call
50-55	1:47	End of conversation
	1:50	Typing
55-58	2:00	Called someone
	2:03	End of conversation
	2:04	Talked with Ellen

HODEL FILE

FEBRUARY 18, 1950

TIME	SPOOL # 1	OFFICERS ON DUTY
		Crowley - LAPD
12:30A	Radio plane. Lady sobbing. Hodel asked, "Do you know Charles Smith. Did you know Mr. Usher?". Hodel mentioned something about during the trial. Mentioned what housekeeper knows. "Did you know ? committed suicide"? "Does your husband know your here. Where were you going? (He was questioning her and it sounded like he was repeating her answer as if writing down her answer)	
1:15A	Lady reciting poetry. Hodel says something about an affair with Dr. Hodel. "Relax. Let's finish these two." Joe comes in room. Sounds like objects dropping on floor. Crashing noises.	
1:45A	"Good night Joe".	
2:00A	All quiet.	

TIME	SPOOL # 2	OFFICERS ON DUTY
2:00P		F. Hronek-D.A's Office
2:10P	In bathroom.	
2:50P	Out of bathroom.	
3:26P	Phone ringing four times. Picked up - not answered.	
3:27P	Answered.	
3:31P	Conversation with some lady about the house.	
3:51P	Conversation with the lady.	
4:00P		J. McGrath-D.A's Office
4:20P	Noise around the house. Woman asking for Operator several time Sounded as though she was crying.	
4:22P	No sound.	

HODEL CASE - 🖐

4:25P   Woman asking for operator again. Said something not heard.to
             operator.

4:26P   No noise.

4:35P   Someone walking around.

5:18P   Man and woman talking. Could not understand.

6:05P   Man and woman talking for a few minutes. (Approx. 2) Could not
             understand. They then left the room.

6:15P   Man and woman talking. Garbled.

6:30P   "Is Joe here. Joe is here, wait outside".

6:50P   Man and woman talking. Woman asked the man a question. Unable
             to understand. He answered, "Haven't been able to find it yet.
             Must be around somewhere".

7:07P   Someone using a typewriter.

7:08P   Phone rang - Hodel said, "OK, right away, good".

7:15P   Someone typing.

7:35P   Conversation between two men. Recorded.

Hodel and man with a German accent had a long conversation;
reception was poor, and conversation hard to understand. The
following bits of conversation, however, were overheard.

Hodel to the German - "This is the best pay off I've seen between Law Enforcement Agencies. You do not have the right
connections made." Hodel states,"I'd like to get a connection
made in the D.A.'s office.".

General conversation between the two - "Any imperfections will
be found. They will have to/made perfect. Don't confess ever.
Two and two is not four.". Much laughter. "Were just a couple
 of smart boys". More laughter.

HODEL FILE - 6/

5

Hodel then-in exact detail- explained to the German about his wife being stopped on Wednesday morning by McGrath and Morgan of the District Attorney's office when they stopped her going up her steps to the house on Franklin. It should be noted that every question asked of Mrs. Hodel was repeated ver-batum by Hodel to this German. He then began to explain to the German about his recent trial - making statements that "Ther'e out to get me. Two men in the D.A.'s officer were transferred and de-moted because of my trial. " Hodel then explained about his being questioned at the D.A.'s office on Wednesday morning, and told in great detail as to questions perpounded to him at that time. One statement made to the German was as follows: "Supposin' I did kill the Black Daliah. They couldn't prove it now. They can't talk to my Secretary anymore because she's dead." As stated, heretofore, conversation was garbled, and it was difficult to maintain a line of continuity of conversation. Hodel also referred to a woman in Camarillo. Conversation also referred to Communist. One point of the conversation was also "Have you heard from Powers". The man with the German acent then asked Hodel something about smoking. Hodel said, "I can't afford it - don't smoke". The German said, "I can get it for you Does the Name Hernandez mean anything to you". Hodel then talked to the German about a Furniture store on East 5th Street, where the cops come in and buy lengerie for twenty to fifty dollars. There was much laughter at this point.

8:20P   Sounded as though the two men went down steps and entered the basement and began digging. Something was referred to "Not a trace". It also appeared as though a pipe was being hit.

HODEL FILE - 1   6   OFFICERS ON DUTY
                                             J. McGrath-D.A.'s office

8:25P   Woman screamed.

8:27P   Woman screamed again. It should be noted that a woman was not
           heard before the time of screaming since 6:50PM. She was not
           in any conversation, and not heard of again until the time of
           letting out these two screams.

NOTE: Officer Crowley, LAPD, arrived for duty at 7:45 PM while the
           above mentioned conversation was taking place. His log is as
           follows:

7:45P   Hodel talking to a man with an accent, possibly German. "Telephone
           men were here. Operator ? Realize there was nothing I could do
           put a pillow over her head, and cover her with a blanket. Get
           a taxi. Call Georgia Street Receiving Hospital right away.
           Expired at 12:39. They though there was something fishy. Any-
           way, now they may have figured it out. Killed her. Maybe I
           did kill my Secretary. They must have enough on him to be guilty
           or he wouldn't have confessed. Time for research (Lots of
           pounding). FBI were over to see me too, three weeks ago.

8:35P   Above man talking - possible German accent. "Two years since.
           regardless of what happens. Police." Much laughter.

8:40P   Above man leaves the house escorted to the door by Hodel.

8:50P   Hodel makes telephone call (Very plain) "Are you party ad-
            vertised for the studio. I have the paper here now. If you'll
           come over I'll be glad to show it to you. On Franklin, near
           Normandy. Your a painter ?" I always have a painter, sculptor,
           or artist of some type here. It's that kind of a house. It's
           a wing of this house. Phone me just before you come, NO 27464,
           and I'll be sure to be in. The name is Hodel, 5123 Franklin Ave.
           Your name - Karbert. If you'll call me, I'll be glad to show you
           the place".

9:25P   Maid questioning Hodel about her citzenship and what the
             immigration officers say in regards to her father. Hodel talking
             about a drunken judge in a pink shirt deciding the technicality
             of the law as far as her citzenship is concerned. Maids
             citizenship papers are fowled up (improper entry). Subject to
             deportation. Going to have a waver of documents (1947) They'll
             realize you acted in good faith. Hodel says, "are you hungry to
             go across the border?"

9:50P   Writing on typewriter.

10:00P   Turned on radio - unable to detect conversation.

10:45P   Walking - opened drawers. Started typing.

10:50P   Telephone rang. (Recorded)
             "Hello Muriel, how are you dear? I'm not doing anything. (laughi
             I don't know of any amnesia that you have. I have had some since
             you were here. A couple of princesses dropped in. I took them
             to the Burbank to a burlesque-they really enjoyed the show.
             Why don't you drop by and talk to me about it sometime.

11:00P   Typing until 11:15 (steady)

11:15P   (Put on spool #4)
             No conversation until 12:10AM. Spoke to lady. (Unable to hear
             what said). Apparently working at his desk, sounds of paper and
             drawers.

FEBRUARY 19, 1950   SPOOL #4   OFFICERS ON DUTY
                                               Crowley - LAPD

12:12A   Typing.

12:17A   Conversing with lady few words (Did not get).

HODEL FILE - 4

8

12:25A   Walking and conversation with lady. (Recorded) (Maybe lady

              caller)

Spool Time

0-60 -SPOOL #4

12:35A   Radio still interfering. Unable to get any of the conversation.

12:40A   Lots of laughing and talking. "Don't make my drink too strong".

12:41A   Female voice - "Well I'll be darned." "Hodel-They are just

              trying ------?"

12:55A   Still talking to this lady - Recording it but radio too loud to

              hear conversation.

12:55A   George - Yes.

1:20A   Still recording conversation - Unable to pick it up over the

              interference of the radio.

1:21A   Girl - "You know my mother doesn't like it one bit".

              Hodel - "Champagne creeps up on you".

1:25A   Mentions Brown Derby restaurant.

              END OF SPOOL #4

SPOOL #5

1:28A   (Sounds like friendly conversation with lady friend, and nothing

              pertinent to investigation) "Lovey Dovey" tone of voice.

1:42A   Walking in house.

1:43A   Girl in bathroom. She answers "Yes" to another part of the hous

1:45A   Talking in the distance. Then conversation ceases.

              NOTE: Officer Brechel who relieved me came past Hodel's reside

              at 1:45AM. He observed a girl and a fellow (approx. 25 to 30 y

              leaving Hodel's house. They got in a 1936 Hudson sedan,

              license 19E 804, man driving, went W on Franklin. There is als

              a Fleetline Chevrolet about a 1946 grey or light green Ill.

              license 1303245 parked in front of the house.

HODEL FILE - ⁄⁄

9

1:47A	In bathroom.
1:50A	Typing.
2:20A	Hodel says, "You better go to bed". Lady (probably maid) arguing. Hodel says, "youv'e been here 5 hours - You don't have to go through everything.
2:48A	Typing - He/^{del}said, "just wipe off table by ashtray. I'll move the tobacco (someone wiping desk) more typing
2:54A	Woman's voice. "I think I'll get everything". Hodel, "Yes please". Woman's voice. "I'll dust here too".
2:58A	Hodel. "You better go to bed Ellen". Typing stopped, radio turned off. Went to Lavatory and urinated.
3:00A-3:30	Whistling, moving around, then all quiet.
3:45A	Snoring.
7:30A	Faint buzzer. Man's voice very faintly, probably outside door opened momentarily. Very loud, street noises. Hodel still asleep.
8:00A	J. McGrath-D.A.'s Office
10:20A	A.M. phone rang - talked to someone(personal) about coming over later in the day.
11:50A	Hodel up and around, noise in bathroom.
12:00P	Jemison-D.A.'s Office.
12:45P	Answered phone. "How long you going to be in town. I'm busy this P.M. How about this evening. Let me get in touch with Dorothy first".
12:50P	Typing 10 minutes.
12:55P	Hodel on phone says "This is Hodel. I'm going to stay around" and hangs up. "I'm listening to music" to woman's voice inquir, "The soloist is up at Camarillo".

12:55P   "Do we have any extra blankets"Ellen---"No we have sheets only". Hodel - "Oh we havent".

1:06P   Hodel on phone - "We'll work it out some way. Do you get off in Hollywood or Beverly Hills?" Balance not distinguished.

1:10P   Hodel-"He will be here tonite and may stay until tomorrow. You'd better make up a bed for him anyway".

1:45P   Phone rings - No conversation. ALL QUIET.

1:50P - 1:55P   Phone rings - Recorded. Hodel - "Where are you now. Sunset & Cornel. Then come to 5121 Franklin". "Yes, sure I'll do it". Hangs up.

2:00P   Hear conversation in distance or Hodel quoting poetry.

2:05P   S.M. 42421. Hodel asked for this number. "Hello Kenny, let me talk to Mrs. Hodel.

2:05P to 2:08P   Recorded. Conversation. Hodel and Mrs. Hodel. "Hello dear. How's everything. Kids alright. How's everything else? Oh, yes dear, I thought I'd come down and bring that to you that you asked for. Kenneth Rexerall called me today, your friend. Should I bring him down to your house this evening. Have you a snack for us. I'll be there at 6 or 6:30 with Kenneth. We'll leave here at 5 or 5:30.

2:12P   Sit down and relax "Kenny". But you can't pin that on me. So you come down to see Ryder. He's a collector that guy. He works for N.B.C.

2:14P   Recorded. Mr. Ryder is sure queer. Hodel-are you addressing a mass meeting or what? You'll have to sleep in the housekeeper's room. She's about this high. Laughter. "Oh we've had some dillys. Discusses chiropractors. "I don't think Dorothy cares. She has a great big living room.

HODEL FILE - ⊕   <u>OFFICERS ON DUTY</u>
                                                            Jemison-D.A.'s office
                                    11

2:25P   Jimmy Fitzimmons made notes. "Where are these things? What's
             the name of the poem? Sounds of auto crash in street.

Off 2:29P   Both leave and return. Kenny - Exfloius immortality. Hodel-
             "What have been doing besides writing. Kenny - "Traveling".

On 2:31P   Hodel - "Did you get to Cine and the Orient."

             Kenny - "No, went to England."

             Unable to hear - laughter.

Off   Kenny - "You can make a lot of money in Paris. I was in Western
2:35   Europe about 1 year.

2:38P   Hodel - "Did they pay your expenses". Laughter. "Hodel
             was it hard making ends meet". Kenny-"No, not so bad". Hodel-
             "He's a sexual character. Proably decayed bodies caused the
             rancid odors and back ground setting in the orient, in Hongkong"
             Hodel discusses Chinese food.

2:40P   Peter Chang on Sunset Strip has the best. Was big shot in China
             Kenny-"You can't believe the terrible food situation in
             England".

2:45P   Hodel-"They gave a banquet and I had an interpreter and the
             American Guard." Laughter. "It takes a couple months to
             get thru to Hankow. Kenny-"I always wanted to see Central Asia,
             but the war has been going on since the 39's."
             Hodel-"Jean Lamb spent several years in Peiping. His
             reports would be on desks of Cinese war lords as soon as on the
             desk of the Ambassador. He was a staff officer. He then
             was employed by a War Lord. 100's of cases of wrist watches.]
             was bribery on a big scale. They had internal war. He was
             ushered in and here was a yellow silk drapery. He spoke Chinese

HODEL FILE -

12

OFFICERS ON DUTY
Jemison-D.A.'s office

2:45P perfectly. He met Prime Minister Hang Chow.

2:55P Jean became a great power and spent 7 years there. He was out here. I tried to negotiate with him. Hodel-"They have a special variety of pictures".

Spool Time Kenny-"Yes!

3:00-3:00P Phone rings. Recorded. Hodel-"Yes, I will", and hangs up.

Off- 3:03 3:05P Phone rings. No conversation. All Quiet.

3:15P Walking sounds

3:20P Hodel conversation with Ellen.
Ellen - "Mr. Hodel". Hodel-"Uh huhhuh".

3:25P All Quiet.

3:30P Hodel and Kenny? Converse. Hodel-"Will you have tea or sherry?
Kenny - "Tea"
"Sipping of tea" sound.
Kenny-"This man is a heart special. He is Dr. Roth. I was to the doctor in San Diego.
Hodel - "Read thru this, then we can discuss it more intelligently Hodel laughs. "It has some coverage. I'm selling my art collection Monday and Tuesday, and I'm then taking off for Asia." Kenny-I am in process of breaking up with my wife of 15 years. No children".
Hodel-"I have 3 boys. You'll see them later. Dorothy lives here a while, and then takes off". Kenny-"What about M".
Hodel-"She is on staff of San Francisco Chronicle. Art Editor. had a serious operation.

HODEL FILE - 13

OFFICERS ON DUTY
Jemison-D.A.'s office

Spool
Time

On 3:45 -3:40P   Laughter.

Hodel-"How were they? They had great masses of hair

those whores. He was a

Hodel-"Rosey at 555 Hyde St., San Francisco, was a whor

but a honey."

Kenny-"I knew a tall one-black hair like Hollywood Blac

hair, pale pale gray eyes. I took her home. I thru

her in the bath tub - she was drunk. I massaged her.

rubbed her under the belly. I got 2 or 3 phone calls.

She got mixed up with some bad people. She called and

said the Psychiatrist was treating her. I guess I

Off 3:52-3:52P   am spoiled (Sounded tight) Dames I know all turn out

to be psychiatrists with pale gray eyes.

K. "Dr. Burns would object to your help but he gave

400 to 600 penicillen, but the real help will come fro

you." Hodel-Wouldn't he object to you coming to my ca

On
3:56

        3:58P   K. "No, as you specialize in heart and you are my

friend. (Recorded)

        4:00P   Hodel-"Well alright.

        4:00P   Hronek-D.A.'s office

32-40   4:16P   Conversation with the patient.

40-44   4:30P   Another conversation with a man.

44-46   4:36P   Phone ringing - Hodel answers.

46-47   4:38   Very bad reception of conversation (3 men)

47-48   4:50P   Someone came in - a woman - Let's go in the other room

talking about the house.

HODEL FILE - 42   OFFICERS ON DUTY
                                                                   Hronek, D.A.'s office
Spool   14
Time
48-62   4:54P   Talking with a man about some special treatment

                      apparently syphilis and marital troubles.

SPOOL #6 5:20P   Continuation of previous conversation.
0-6
         5:37P   The man leaves with the instructions to call Wednesday.

         5:45P   Typewriter at work. Looking for something in the desk.

6-15   5:49P   Another man came in - talking about some girl.

15-21   6:03P   Phone rang - answered - continuation of conversation.

21-24   6:11P   Making a call - no answer.

24-33   6:27P   Conversation with his buddy. Mostly females.

         6:30P   Everything quiet.

         7:22P   Phone rang 9X   No answer.

                                                         Crowley-LAPD

         7:45P   All quiet.

         8:45P   Dog barks.

         9:15P   Someone enters. Walking and noises in house.

         9:30P   Dog barking.

         9:35P   Walking in house - dog barking.

         9:36P   Lady talking in the distance.

         9:37P   Walking near "Mike".

        10:05P   Dog barks.

        11:00P   Telephone rings 4 times (No one answered)

FEBRUARY 20, 1950   BRECHEL-LAPD

         2:00A   All quiet from 11 PM until 2 AM.

         2:00A-8:00A All is quiet.

FEBRUARY 20, 1950   SPOOL #6   OFFICER ON DUTY

                                                        J. McGrath, D.A.'s
                                                                Office

Spool Time

	8:00A	No noise at all around house.
	9:30A	No noise or activity.
	9:40A	Phone rang 12 times - no answer.
	9:41A	Phone rang 12 times - no answer.
	10:40A	Someone enters - walking and noises in house.
	10:48A	Phone rings 3 times - answered by Ellen. Took message - stated Hodel will be in 2 PM.
	11:20A	Ellen enters - turns on radio - mexican program.
	11:35A	Much noise in room - sounds like sweeping - no conversation

                                                        Sullivan, D.A.'s
                                                                Office
                                                            12 noon

	1:00P	All quiet.
	1:15P	Telephone - 4 times - answered by maid - "You his father? He went to beach last nite - said he'd be here early today". No further conversation.
	1:35P	Phone - 3 times - answered by maid - no conversation.
	2:00P	Quiet.
	2:20P	Walking around - maid singing - banging noises.
	2:23P	Quiet.
	2:35P	Phone rings - 2 times.
	2:45P	Someone entered - walked around very fast.
33-42	3:00P	Door bell rings - answered by Hodel.
		Talking to unknown woman - Dials phone - Asks for some woman - Unable to hear name - Talk about renting rooms over phone - Attempting to get this one party to take both rooms - Hung up - Made another phone call - Wrong number.

HODEL FILE - 16

Spool
Time

	3:10P	Walks around house - water running.
42-44	3:12P	Phone rings - answered by Hodel - Unable to identify who he was talking to.
	3:14P	Whistling and rustling of papers.
44-45	3:25P	Phone rings - answered by Hodel.
		Looks for phone # TR 1252.
45-45½	3:28P	Phone rings - answered by Hodel - Unable to connect conversation.
45½-46	3:30P	Phone - Answered by Hodel. Called person on other end "Baby Doll".
	3:45P	Stanton - Crime Lab here; working on set to eliminate hum.
	4:00P	Talking to maid - something about post office, unintelligible - typewriter going.
	4:01P	Machine off - being worked on by Stanton.
	4:08P	Machine back in operation - typing.
	4:09P	Phone rings - "Rex Kane mentioned - Mr. Butlers name mentioned "What 2 boxes represent - Will get a little more information - Will call back".
	4:15P	Walter Morgan - D.A.'s office relieves
46-50	4:20P	Conversation - 27464 - gave number of his phone.
	4:21P	Telephoned - conversation unintelligible - airplane passing passing over.
	4:22P	Talking to maid - "Close to Mexico".

HODEL FILE - 18

17

SPOOL #7
Spool
Time

	4:25P	Spool #7
	4:30P	Typewriter noise.
	4:35P	Unintelligible conversation with maid.
	4:48P	Telephone rang - was answered by Hodel - short conversation about price of tea.
	4:58P	Began typing.
0-1	5:05P	Conversation with maid - Typing.
1-3.5	5:08P	" " " "
3.5-5	5:14P	" " " "
5-6	5:16P	" " " "
6-8	5:18P	" " " "
8-11	5:28P	Telephone rang - answered by Hodel - conversation about "Units".
11-27.5	5:45P	Telephone rang - answered by Hodel - conversation about crime prevention; Delinquent accounts; Dr. E.W. DeLong's October 1948 account; Blood and spinal fluids; employment of Collector; Hodel's stock ownership in a company - maid entered conversation about time; Hodel stated that it was six o'clock, that he had to leave at seven, that he would be back at twelve - begins to type.
27.5-28.5	6:13P	Noise like writing on paper.
28.5-29.5	6:18P	Hodel asked maid to close door.

HODEL FILE -

18

Spool Time

Spool	Time	
29.5-30.5	6:20P	Telephone rang - answered by Hodel - asked what the score was - ended with goodnight.
30.5-34	6:27P	Hodel asked for Sycamore 60647 (Unrecorded) - Gave operator Olympia 3476; Asked for Cris; Conversation about taking place; Hodel has another party anxious to take place - ended with "So Long".
34-42	6:23P	Dialing of phone - Hodel asked for Mrs. Montgomery - conversation about getting place in one or two days, "Just a minute, hold on", pause in conversation- Desk noise - continued conversation - ended with "Good Nigh
	6:52P	Hodel said "Already, O.K."(Not Recorded)
42-44.5	6:53P	Hodel said "Get some from _____"
	6:55P	Hodel said, "O.K. be right with you" (Not Recorded)
44.5-45	6:56P	Desk noise - Hodel walking away - door slams.
	7:20P	Stanton changed recorders.
45-45.5	7:30P	Shower noise
	8:00P	Crowley, LAPD, on duty, relieves Morgan, D.A.
	8:10P	Walking in house.
	8:18P	Walking - door slams.
	8:30P	Walking in house.
	8:35P	Loud noises in desk.
	8:40P	Someone turns radio on.
	8:45P	Crowley and Morgan note that phone # OL 3476 that Hodel charged call to at 6:27PM this date differed from # NO 27464 which he gave at 8:50PM, on 2-18-50. (He gave # 27464 to the party who was inquiring about renting the

19

Spool
Time

studio, gave the address as 5123 Franklin Ave.) Morgan
dialed the above OL 3476 from this telephone, and Hodel
answered "Hello". (Morgan can positively identify the
voice). Morgan asked, "Is this OL 3746", and Hodel
answered, "No, this is OL 3476", to which Morgan replied
"I'm sorry, I have the wrong number". Crowley was unable
to hear any sound whatsoever from Hodel's residence during
this conversation - Crowley then called Lt. Hale at
Business Office, and was informed that OL 3476 is a
non published secret number, registered to Dr. George
Hodel at 5121 Franklin Ave.

9:00P	Alls quiet except for radio (playing classical music).
9:07P	Door closes.
9:10P	Lady talking in distance (sounds like maid's voice) It sounded as though she said "are there any more cops around". Heard no answer. (Not Recorded) End of conversation.
9:49P	Walking - door closes.
9:55P	Walking - other noises.
10:07P	Radio - stops playing.
10:25P	Door closes - walking - turns radio on - changes stations then turns it off.
10:40P	All quiet.
10:47P	Someone moving around. Doors open - close. More walking.
11:00P	Bound of someone's movements in house.

HODEL FILE -

Spool
Time

	11:24P	Door slams - someone's movements in house - goes to bathroom-urinates.
	11:45P	Walking in house - radio turned on.
	11:55P	Minngapolis Symphony orchestra playing. Station KFAC.
	12:30A	Door closes - radio still playing.
	12:55A	Walking in house.
	1:05A	Radio stops playing.
	1:07A	Loud noises in desk - walking.
	1:25A	Walking in house.
	1:45A	All quiet.
	1:49A	Walking in house.
	1:50A	Brechel, LAPB, on duty, relieves Crowley
45.5-49.00	2:15A	Loud noises. Hodel talking to maid. Hodel-"I never found your keys. Have you looked for them?" Maid, "Yes".
Off	2:20A	Hodel at desk going thru papers. cusses, to himself. Sorting of papers in desk.
	2:30A	Still sorting papers. Closes drawer. Opens other drawer. Searching for something in desk.
	2:35A	Hodel goes to lavatory. Urinates.
	2:40A	Hodel in bedroom with someone, probably Ellen. Hodel - "No use working hard". Other whispered conversati unable to make out. Hodel goes in bathroom - runs water.
	2:45A	Conversation with Ellen.
49.00-51.25	2:45A	Whispered conversation - recorded. Loud noises. Unable to make out conversation.

HODEL FILE - 26   21

FEBRUARY 21, 1950

Spool
Time

51.25- 54.00	2:55A	Noises at desk. Hodel speaking, unable to make out due to pounding noise.
	3:10A	Sounds of numerous drawers opening and closing in different parts of the house.
	3:25A	Sounds of walking about the house.
	3:30A	Movements in house cease.
	3:45A	Alls quiet. Snoring (Hodel in bedroom)
	4:50A	Snoring ceases - alls quiet.
	5:00A	Some disconnected noises. Hodel tossing in bed or reading.
	5:45A	Hodel yawns and resumes snoring.
	6:05A	Snoring ceases - alls quiet.
	6:45A	Snoring resumes.

```
HODEL FILE -                        22

FEBRUARY 21, 1950, 8:00 AM                      J. McGrath, D.A.'s offic
                                                      on duty
```

Spool Time		
49-50	10:55A	Telephone rang - answered by Hodel - said "Hello" then began to walk around and make a lot of noise.
50-55	11:00A	Conversation - sounds like Ellen arguing - unable to hear while recorder on.
	11:10A	Changing wire - doubt if conversation was recorded.
	11:10A	No conversation - just loud noise in house.
SPOOL 8		Started 11:15 AM
	11:20A	Conversation between Hodel and Ellen - unable to understand - not recording - can't tell if recorder is working.
	11:30A	Conversation - Hdel and Ellen.
0-4	11:30A	Telephone answered by Hodel - gave directions to other part Attempting to rent room
4-7	11:40A	Telephone - answered by Hodel - unable to identify other party.
	11:50A	Telephone conversation - garbled.
7-9½	11:50A	Sullivan - D.A.'s office on duty
	12:00noon	Hear Hodel muttering to himself.
9½-10	12:15P	Testing by Neblo Crime Lab.
10-11½	12:50P	Conversation with Ellen - unintelligible - "I like potatoes".
	12:55P	Moving around - noises
	1:00P	Bad hum in set - Ellen talking but unintelligible.
10½-19		Words between Dr. and maid, "I would call American Counsel if I had money. Discussing her citizenship problems. Mai doing considerable talking - unintelligible.

HODEL FILE - ~~2d~~

23

Spool
Time

	1:10P	Typewriter operating.
19-22	1:15P	Conversation by maid - much noise.
to		
22½	1:20P	Conversation by maid with Hodel.
	1:30P	Noises in room - considerable hum on receiver.
22½-26	1:31P	Conversation between Hodel and Mail - regarding Mexico.
	1:40P	Sounds like water running for past 4 or 5 minutes. Can hear Hodel's voice in background but unintelligible.
	1:55P	Hodel muttering, and water running.
	2:20P	Typewriter.
26-33	2:21P	Phone - Doctor answerax - talks about architecture - talking about selling house.
33-35	2:25P	Typing
	2:55P	Conversation between Hodel and Maid. Complaining of having to do housework.
	3:05P	Typing.
	3:15P	Typing continues.
	3:30P	Hear maid talking in background - hum in set continues.
35-38	3:35P	Hodel and maid talking. Unintelligible due to hum.
38-39	3:38P	Conversation with maid (Recorded).
		Ended recording - nothing being said.
39-40	3:40P	Hodel and maid talking.
	3:48P	Typing
	4:00P	Crime lab boys here - working on hum.
	4:00P	Hronek - D.A.'s office relieving Sullivan

SPOOL 9

	4:20P	L.A.P.D. lab men left.

HODEL FILE - 🖫

24

SPOOL
TIME

0-4	4:36P	Phone rang - Hodel answers (Patient)
	4:40P	Starts typing again.
4-16	4:44P	Phone rang - Hodel answers.
	4:55P	Starts typing again.
	5:32P	Typing stopped
	5:45P	Typing resumed
	6:15P	Typing stopped - Hodel moving around in the background.
	8:00P	Lewis, LAPD, relieving Hronek (Spool time 16)
	8:17P	Phone rang twice - no one answered.
	8:50P	Radio playing - station KFAC
	9:30P	Radio - still playing - classical music.
	10:45P	Radio off
16-22	10:47P	Maid on phone wants to talk to American Counsel in Mexico. Gave OL phone (Recorded)
	11:10P	Someone went toilet - No further talking on phone. Call never completed.
	11:15P	Radio started playing.
	12:10A	Radio turned off.
	12:35A	Someone walking about house.
	12:50A	Heard Hodel voice first time tonite - "Said leave that on".
	1:15A	A lady gave big "Ho-Hum" also lots of noise like slaming drawers and prying lids off of Wooden boxes. Also sawing.
	1:45A	Hodel told Maid she had better go to bed.

5 minutes - wire used - 2 PM end watch for Lewis

HODEL FILE - 🆖
FEBRUARY 22, 1950   25

Spool
Time

	2:00A	<u>Brechel, LAPD on duty</u>
	2:10A	Hodel and Ellen enter room.
22- 40	2:12A	Hodel - "Will you leave that light on there, I'm just a little nervous". Hodel- "I suppose its asking a little too much". Conversation with Ellen recorded. Hodel - "What that you got there". Whistling. Hodel- "Thats a lot of nonsense". Ellen talks back. Water runnir Hodel has conversation with Ellen - asks if something is too difficult. Hodel says he is worried. Hodel - "You don't need this razor". Ellen - "Maybe you better leave it".
	2:20A	Conversation regarding cutting garment and sending it to laundry. Recorded.
	2:23A 2/2🆖	Hodel asks if red coat is still at cleaners. Ellen thinks she sees it (apparently both are searching a closet) Conversation recorded.
	2:25A	Hodel is asking Ellen if she can stitch. Ellen replies she knows well enough. Ellen admires a chinese box. Hodel says a manchurian princess gave it to him. He says he
	2:27A	is going to sell it. Ellen asks for taste.
Off	2:29A	Ellen wants to stay with him, he tells her to go to bed, she can stay with him tomorrow.
	2:32A	Movements around room. Low conversation unable to make out
	2:35A	Deep breathing. Hodel and Ellen probably having inter-course.

HODEL FILE - ▓▓

FEBRUARY 22, 1950

Spool
Time

40-43	2:40A	Ellen says she wants to go now. Hodel says she should have gone to her room. He is pretty well tired. Sounds
off		indicates movements on bed.
43-49.5	2:45A	Deep breathing. Movements on bed.
		Definite sounds of climax of intercourse. Hodel sighs loudly and passionately.
	2:49A	Hodel and Ellen talking. Ellen wants him to stay with her all night. She begs him. He says no, he is tired.
Off	2:51A	Alls quiet.
	3:10A	Sounds of light snoring. Not Hodel.
	3:40A	Sounds indicate someone moving about.
	3:45A	Alls quiet.
49.5 to 51.5	7:55A	Phone is dialed. Hodel does not speak, but a female voice on phone is not distinct (recorded). This may be Ellen
off		using kitchen phone as Hodel not up yet.
	8:10A	Hodel arises, goes to lavatory.
	8:00A	J. McGrath - D.A.'s office on duty
	8:33A	Phone rings - Hodel answers - told someone to write to Consumers Research, Washington New Jersey, Hung up.
51.5- 53.5	8:35A	Conversation with Ellen - could not understand (recorded)
	9:08A	Very heavy breathing or gasping by Hodel as if a nervous dream. About 6 times.
53.5- 56	9;55A	Phone rang - Hodel answered - recorded. Said will borrow some money and send you $10.00. Said he would try to come down and get the fish.

27

HODEL FILE - 26

FEBRUARY 22, 1950

SPOOL 10

Spool
Time

	10:30A	Put on Spool #10
0-10.8	10:47A	Phone call - Hodel answered - recorded - Hodel did little talking - just kept stating, "Uh-huh" "Uh-huh" Did you see Dr. Burns since I've see you. Does he feel I'm interfering? Hope he does not resent - talking to Theodore - said when reports comes at 1 PM today or tomorrow will contact you - When we won't be disturbed.
	11:00A	Hodel urinated - took shower.
	11:23A	Hodel typing.
	11:50A	Hodel said "Let's see the phone is CR 5527 or 5537 Ellen phoned and said, are you open tonight. "Oh after 6" Then Hodel said to Ellen you go tomorrow night, at 9 PM.
	12:00noon	Morgan on duty.
	12:10P	Unintelligible conversation between two men (Hodel and ?- 2 minutes).
	12:21P	Hodel - "There must be something" Ellen - "There isn't anything" Hodel- "I'm pretty sure there is something". Recorded.
	12:26P	Hodel - "Straighten up that room in there - just the way it was before".
10.8- 14.6	12:35P	Telephone rang - Hodel - "Oh yeah Power - are you in town - good - things are sort of busy right now for the next ten days - we're tapped now again - well there is pretty much going on regarding yourself and me - I was questioned about you and so forth - maybe you can find out - Don't you know

HODEL FILE - 27

FEBRUARY 22, 1950

<u>Spool</u>
<u>Time</u>

	12:35P	someone up there? Maybe you can find out what the hell is going on up there. I would like to see you in person when we get a chance - what's your phone? That's your new phone? (Ends) "OK - so long".
14.6- 16.8	12:58P	Telephone rang - Hodel - "Hello, yeah, yeah, yeah". Pause - "yeah, yeah, that's the only thing to tell em - don't say a single thing - who was it? - Sullivan? be polite, be very nice but say you can't tell em a thing without your laywer's advice. O.K.".
16.8-17		Blank.
17-18.5	1:10P	Conversation between Hodel and Ellen (unintelligible) Noise - airplane noise.
18.5- 19.5	1:36P	Conversation between Hodel and Ellen (partly unintelligible
	2:00P	Hodel in bathroom - running water.
19.5- 24	2:32P	Telephone rang - Hodel - conversation about sales "What sort of a place did you find? In Santa Monica? Conversation about $1320. "I already sent him a letter - see you maybe over the week end" (Ends "O.D. Dad")
24-25	2:54P	Telephone rang - Hodel - I can't call you back? Can you call me from an outside phone? Call you back where you are now in about ten minutes.
	4:00P	Only sound is from radio playing, station KFAC. <u>Not</u> <u>recorded</u>. ~~ERICKSON~~ BROWNSON on duty, <u>4:00 PM</u> Occasional sound of a person moving about the room.

HODEL FILE - 28

FEBRUARY 22, 1950

Spool
Time

25	8:00P	Lewis on duty - radio playing
25- 27.5	9:00P	Hodel come in room - talks to maid "Low" She wants to know what happened - he did not answer. Radio still playing (Recorded)
27.5- 30.6	9:24P	Phone rang - maid answered - said Chris is here. (Recorded No word yet. "Could hear someone whistling. Radio real loud. Could not make out what else was said.
30.6- 35.8	9:40P	Phone rings 3 times - maid said call half hour - no more talking - someone in toilet - flush same. Some one walking xxxxxxxx heavy and fast - radio - still playing.
35.8- 37.5	10:10P	Phone rang - maid answers. (Recorded) What was said - but could not make it out as radio still very loud.
	10:34P	Hodel yelled - is that door locked. Maid answered, "No do you want to come in" Hodel said "No" Maid said, "Why did you want to know" (No answer)
	11:28P	Radio turned off - everything quiet.
	1:45A	Hodel walk about house-finally goes to toilet - after using toilet he flushes it, then walks about house again. Slams a door and is talking real low to himself (unable to understand him)
	2:00A	Lewis - end of watch.

XXXXXXXXXXXXXXXX
	2:00A	Brechel, LAPD, on duty
	2:30A	Hodel walking about the bedroom.
	2:30A	Hodel asleep. Snoring. Alls quiet.

HODEL FILE -   30

FEBRUARY 23, 1950

SPOOL #10

Spool
Time

	8:00A	Jim McGrath-D.A.'s Office on duty
	8:55A	Phone ringing - Hodel snoring. Hodel did not wake up to answer - still snoring.
	9:07A	Someone (sounds like womans footsteps) enters room (probably living room).
	9:35A	Phone rang - no answer.
	10:10A	Phone ringing - 8 times - no answer.
	10:12A	Someone walking around - sounds like Hodel - conversation between Hodel and Ellen about going to store. Not recorded.
37-40	10:23A	Conversation with someone by Hodel. Phone did not ring, and he didn't dial, but sounded like phone conversation. (Recorded) Said she is my maid - you know she is peculiar - talked like he was asking for medical help.
40-41	10:27A	(Recorded) Hodel talking - it appears to Telephone Co. complaining about maid making long distance phone calls.
41-44	10:28A	Recorded. Hodel phoned someone asked for $1000.00 cash advance - said he was short of ready cash..
44-44.5	10:35A	Dialed phone - asked for a number - sounded like Insurance #451651.
44.5-48.5	10:41A	Telephone rings - said, "How are you Miss Montgomery - talk about getting a house. Read note he said he found on his desk. Said he will call tomorrow.

HODEL FILE -

Spool
Time

| 48.5-57 | 10:47A | Phone rings - answered by Hodel - asks about a letter - talk about architecture - says he has been selling some antiques - says he will send some money. |

SPOOL #11

0-2	11:05A	Conversation with Ellen - says, "I haven't any money. I will have to sell everything".
2-12	11:09A	Hodel and Ellen (recorded) in a conversation. Regarding Ellens phone calls to the Mexican Consulate. Hodel gave her hell - said to write letters instead of phoning - raised hell about the bills from the Phone Company - also told her to never talk over the phone.
12-14	11:23A	(Recorded) Hodel phones someone (Neeks) Neeks not in.
14-14.5	11:27A	Phone rang - Hodel answered, said "Yes, I'll be there at
14.5-16	11:33A	Hodel and Ellen - talk regarding a form she received about a street car accident - told her to say she did not see anything - throw the form away. (Recorded)
	11:55A	Hodel typing.
	12:00noon	Snyder-Sullivan. D.A's office on duty.
	12:15P	Hodel still typing.
16-18	12:50P	Hodel calls Ellen (recorded) Unintelligible.
	12:52P	Quiet.
	12:55P	Typing.
18-23	1:00P	Phone rings - Hodel answers (recorded) tables and chairs to go - asks for address - expects to give someone money by Wednesday - selling tea.

HODEL FILE -

32

Spool
Time

	1:05P	End of telephone conversation.
23-24	1:10P	Talking to Ellen (recorded)
	1:11P	Hodel typing.
	1:20P	Phone rings - Hodel answers - short - wrong number.
	1:25P	Phone rings - apparently in remote part of house. Could barely hear it.
	1:30P	Hodel talks to Ellen - unintelligible - very few words.
	1:33P	Someone moving furniture around - hell of a racket - (P.S. not recorded) Someone climbing down and up stairs.
24-25½	1:42P	Hodel talks to someone (Recorded)
25½-27	1:45P	Order a suit of blue - talk by a Charlie China type 5121 - conversation by Hodel (recorded) Delivery in about a week.
27-28	1:48P	Hodel calls Department of Commerce - calls information.
	1:50P	Hodel calls on phone (recorded) Will be out 5 or 6 PM (Recorded)
	1:52P	Hodel dials phone - calls Mr. Neeb - wants to go to office Will not be able to this week (not recorded)
28-32	1:55P	Hodel dials phone - Department of commerce (recorded) in regards selling car in Mexico.
32-33	2:05P	Hodel dials phone - car to Mexico City - talks to F.B.I. (recorded)
33-35½	2:07P	Hodel dials phone - in regards purchase of Packard car (recorded) (P.S.-he wants to go to Mexico City) NO 2-7464.
35½-37	2:12P	Phone rings - Hodel answers - in regards Packard car. (recorded)

HODEL FILE -   33

<u>Spool</u>
<u>Time</u>

37-49   2:15P   Phone rings - Hodel answers - Hodel dials phone -
                  talking to "Dear" (Recorded) Want to meet at 4 PM.,
                  at Holly and Sycamore - Garden Grove Apts.

49-52   2:30P   Hodel talks to Ellen - in regards Ellens citizenship.
                  (recorded).

SPOOL #12

0-1   2:40P   Conversation Hodel and maid (recorded) Money for maid.
                  "I don't wany any".

         2:50P   Water running - conversation in background.

         3:00P   Plane passes over.

1-1½   3:05P   Phone rings - Hodel answers "I will call you back on the
                  other phone (recorded)

1½-4½   3:06P   Dials phone - "Is Dr. Hussey there". (recorded) "Are
                  you holding some lot reports for me?"

4½-7½   3:10P   Quiet.

         3:11P   Hodel talking - "What's happened" (Recorded)

         3:12P   Phone rings - no one answers phone. Hodel still talking.
                  "Have you got some sheets and blankets?"

         3:25P   Quiet for past 10 minutes.

         4:00P   All quiet on the Hodel front.

         4:35P   Someone walking around.

         5:15P   Movement around including walking.

         <u>5:18P</u>   <u>Jemison on Duty, D.A.'s office.</u>
                  All quiet.

         <u>6:40P</u>   <u>Hronek, D.A.'s office on duty</u>

         6:45P   Hear movements, footsteps in the house.

         7:35P   Radio on, very loud.

HODEL FILE -

Spool Time		
26-28.5	10:36P	Someone knock - Hodel said, come in - some man entered unable to understand onnversation.
28.5-59.5	10:44P	Hodel and some man sounds like talking about going fishing or about pictures of fish - lot of noise. Talking about fastest bird - animal and fish and hos fast they are. Hodel - "Were going to try to get the big house out here. skid-row - Pasadena - case of Bowron - Dug out - can't stay forever. Don't know - Well "Tom" - Police Department My moving from house - 3 very large bedrooms - There are twelve bedrooms. Pasadena - Santa Monica - (Talking about houses) 25,000 - 30,000. The grounds are kind of deteriorated. I have to use the car.
	11:30P	Radio playing.
	12:05A	Walking-noises at desk.
	12:35A	Typing - radio playing.
	12:46A	Hodel and maid speak a few words - cannot understand.
	1:02A	Radio turned down. (Volume)
	1:15A	Walking - Hodel and Ellen in conversation (distance)
	1:25A	Walking
	1:45A	Hodel and Ellen talking (unable to hear) Something about a model.
	1:51A	Typing.

STEVE HODEL

HODEL FILE -

36

SPOOL #13

Spool
Time

	1:55A	Lewis, LAPD on duty.
0-1.5	2:15A	Hodel and maid talking. Hodel asked, "Did you look in the little box in there.
	2:20A	Hodel using typewriter - radio playing.
1.5-3 Wire broke	2:25A	Phone rang - Hodel -"Yes Dear, How are you, what trouble Tell me all about it. I can't understand it. I guess tha finishes it, impossible, see you later.
new wire	2:30A	Hodel says to Maid - You going to bed dear. Hodel now typing.

SPOOL #14

0-1	2:50A	Hodel to maid, "Come on - you better go to bed". Hodel still typing.
	2:55A	Hodel - "You had better go bed now." Maid said, "OK" Hodel said, "Good night sweet". Everything quiet. No more typing.
	3:10A	Door opened - Hodel says "Aren't you going to bed for Chri sake - Hodel yells "O Manuel" Now quiet again.
	3:45A	Hodel snoring.
	6:00A	Everything still quiet.

HODEL FILE - 37

FEBRUARY 24, 1950
SPOOL #14

Spool Time		Sullivan, D.A.'s office on duty
17-19	1:20P	Dials phone (recorded) asks for a new car salesman. What is that car for $1587.00 - How much more with seats in back - $75.00. I've got a 1936 Packard Sedan to trade in. Want to make Packard down payment No chance - Will see you Mr. Shingleton.
	1:25P	Talking to maid - having lunch - maid talks about fis Hodel asks for lemons.
19-20	1:30P	Phone rings - Hodel answers (recorded) "I'll be ther in 15 minutes. Let me come anyway".
	1:31P	Phone rings. Hodel answers (No conversation)
	1:34P	Talks to maid "I got to leave right away".
	1:48P	Phone rings - maid answers - Hodel tells her to tell party he just left.
	1:55P	Phone rings - maid answers - "He will be back in abou 1½ hours".
20-24	2:35P	Someone enters - sounds like maid - answered phone - unable to hear conversation.
	2:38P	Ellen dialed information - asked for number of immigration office - dialed phone - asked to speak to Mr. P----- Apparently out - asked person on phone to have him call her back on NO 27464.

HODEL FILE - 38

Spool
Time

Spool	Time	
	3:15P	Quiet.
	3:25P	Phone rings once - answered apparently in some other part of house.
	3:40P	Phone rings several times - hear no answer.
	3:41P	Phone rings several times - hear no answer.
	3:50P	Phone rings twice - hear no answer.
24-28½	3:55P	Hodel and maid talking - (Recorded). About her citizenship.
	4:00P	**Hronek, D.A.'s office on duty**
28½-30½	4:02P	MU 9077 - Hodel dials over - Is Marian there. Hello dear.
31-34	4:05P	Tries to dial - phone rings - Hodel answered
34-35½	4:07P	Phone rings - Hodel answered. I'd love to have you
35½-36½		when it'll be - around 9 or 10? Operator AT 66402 This is OL 3476
	4:11P	Hello, Mrs. Clark?
	4:20P	Hodel starts typing.
36½-51½	4:25P	Phone rings - Hodel answered - Ellen took over - still talking about the citizenship, Ellen, didn't I tell you not to tell people things over the telephone. Hodel ordered Ellen not to answer any questions over the telephone - Hodel calls NO 27464. Ellen argues with Hodel that lots of people cross the border without papers. Hodel orders the maid not to let anybody in the office. Then starts typing again. Ellen said something about the FBI investigating us.

HODEL FILE * 39

39

Spool
Time

	4:44P	Hodel dials xxx out to some Mr. Blumfield.
	4:50P	Start Spool #15
	4:50P	Typing
	6:14P	Phone rings, stops before Hodel lifts the receiver.
0-1	6:26P	Hodel dials - asks for Lyn report.
1-2½	6:28P	Hodel - Hello Margaret - are you with the patient. I would like for you to stop by - Maybe next week.
2½-8½	6:32P	Hodel dials - What's the number of Holms & Cuttle 7100 Beverly Blvd? Talks about car. What's your name? Anderson - That's easy to remember.
	7:10P	Hear Hodel moving around the house.
	8:00P	Meyer, L.A.P.D. on duty
8½-9½	8:58P	Phone rings. Ellen answers - unable to understand wh or what she says.
9½-31	10:18P	Some girl introduced Hodel to some girl named Mickey talking unable to understand, said something about China tea, two drinks, another man around.
	10:28P	Phone rings - Hodel answers - couldn't understand too well. Come over tomorrow - call before you come after supper some time - have a pencil handy. OL 3476. Good - so am I - will you do that? I will try to keep tomorrow open. (Hangs up) Hodel talks- She graduated from school in Detroit with top honors- what did I have for desert?
	10:35P	Phone rings - Hodel answers - Yes, Why? I would say just forget it all - put some Hillbilly music on - left room, radio on.

SPOOL #15

Spool
Time

31-32½	10:45P	Taling about records - put more records on.
32½-33½	10:49P	Phone rings - Hodel answers - yes, sure, absolutely. I don't really care - just forget the whole thing.
33½-34.2	10:51P	Talk about records again. Put more on.
34½-35	10:55P	Talk about records again. Put more on.
35-36½	11:04P	Girls talking - I only had a glass of tea.
36½-41	11:06P	Girls talking - Hodel talking to girls - lot of noise - radio on loud.
41-42	11:11P	Talking - radio on too loud - can't hear.
42-44½	11:22P	Hodel asks girls if want fire on - turns fire on - girl asks, haven't heard anything further, have you? Someone typing.
44½-45	11:31P	Hodel - reaching for something? Radios on very loud.
45-50	11:40P	Hodel - come here a second. Hear opening desk. Othe girl enters. Girl-"Is this a private conversation? Hodel-"Boy, it is a juicy conversation, what do you want to know". Girl-"I like to be exposed gradually" Hodel-"How ~~many½½x~~ many did you have"? Girl-"52"
	11:51P	Spool ran out on 56. Meyer changed spool - just small talk. couldn't hear too well.

SPOOL #16

1-10	11:57P	Hodel and girl talking - unable to understand. Radio is all can hear.

HODEL FILE - 41

41

Spool
Time

10-11	12:08A	That is Shirley's work.
11-21½	12:10A	Hodel-"Did you ever hear this record?" Played recor sounded like home made, something about humanity??? Played some records of poems. Hodel had recorded.
21½-22½	12:22A	Hodel and girl talking about poems, one girl starts reading poems. Hodel says she is pretty good. Then Hodel reads a poem.
	12:30A	Still reading peems. Hodel and girl. talking about
22½-27	12:39A	poems to read to each other.
27-32	12:45A	Still talking about poems - one girl says she read better then Hodel. One girl read them finish Hodel said "Yes - H - Chrisy" then Hodel said, "I can read better setting by a beauty - noise - then Hodel reads poem.
32-32½	12:51A	Talk about poem he just read, reads some more.
32½-47½	12:58A	Hodel finishes. Girl says - "It is a morbid poem," talk about poem. Hodel says - "you read next one". Talk about records. Hodel says he has some. Girl says "go get them" Sounds like someone leaving. Talk about some onegetting a divorce. Starts reading

again. Hodel - "I own 51% of the stock - talking
about Asia - more small talk - played Chinese soundin
music.

HODEL FILE - 42
FEBRUARY 25, 1950
Spool
Time

42

47½-48½ 1:16A   Talking about records - play some - sounds like a

                cat fight - or a bunch of wash tubs.

48½-50 1:19A   Hodel says something about a sweater looking nice.

                More music - unable to hear talk.

50-56   1:24A   Talk about "Carrey Grey"? Hodel says,"who is that?"

                Bath room and radio on at same time - music - so

                changed spool - then talk about music.

FEBRUARY 25,1950
SPOOL #7

0-27   1:36A   Talking about some place ideal - people from 48 stat

                come - a wonderful oportunity - Santa Barbara one ti

                I waited two years (Hard to hear them) some

                other man talking - "I was guest artist one time".

                Girl - "you can't worry about that". Talking about

                China - Man - "married 4 months. That was enough".

                Hodel comes back in - talk about drawing. Hodel

                says for a beginner is pretty dam good.

27-39   2:00A   <u>Lewis, L.A.P.D. on duty</u>

        2:00A   Big party going on - several girls and men talking.

                Hard to understand but being recorded. Some girl sa

                "Good night Jerry". Party seems to be breaking up

                as everyone is saying Goodnight.

        2:12A   Everything quiet - outside of one person walking

                about room.

39-62   2:14A   Hodel and another man talking about a girl - use to

                be attorney for Barba Sherman. She is wonderful

                dancer - she married a Swiss Counselor. Hodel talki

                about taking girls to South America 3 months - they

                be ready for singing - light opera. I have a way ab

HODEL FILE - 43

Spool
Time

me. I can arrange ti with there folks. I have so
many girls I like to have a rest for awhile. Seem
as though Hodel and this other man are talking about
Traveling with these girls. Hodel said he like to
see parent of each girl and get permission in writing
from them to allow girls to travel. Made arrangement
to meet again Sunday andtalk further on agreements.

End Spool 17
    2:35A

Would like to give it a trial in Mexico City. If you
have girls over Sunday have them bring photograph
of themselves. Talking about they could stay in best
hotels and make at least 2500 per week. Hodel-
"hard job is talking to parents". Hodel says - I
will be the tough guy and you be the great guy. Hode
says - I will have arias. They laugh and Hodel says-
let's go to bed. They leave room and everythings qui
Hodel snoring "And loud".

    3:30A

SPOOL #18

    6:20A   Someone up - walking about house. go into bathroom
and use toilet - then flush same. Then sound like
knocking on a door. Person is Mr. Hodel. Identifiec
by his cough.

    6:30A   Everything quet.

O-5   6:50A   Hodel knocks on Ellen's door - ask "are you up".
She answers "You want in?" He states, "No, I won't
start nothing now - how about 12 o'clock. Huh?"
(part talk recorded)

HODEL FILE - 44   44

Spool
Time

0.5	7:40A	Dog barking as if it had someone cornered.
	8:00A	Lewis, L.A.P.D. off duty
	8:00A	J.McGrath, D.A.'s office on duty
	10:17A	Noise around house - sounded as though someone made a phone call from rear of house. Hodel is up.
	10:28A	Hodel made phone call - asked for"Andy Anderson".
	10:40A	Some man said to Hodel - "Andy Anderson called you". Hodel said to this man - "Tell him I'll call him back
0.5-1	10:42A	Hodel phoned Andy Anderson (recorded) about a car deal of some kind. Hodel said, "Oh no, just send me back my check and I will start fresh".
1-2	11:24A	Hodel phoned (recorded) someone asked if Dr. Bussey there. Gave phone, OL 3476, to call back.
2-4	11:27A	Hodel made phone call - asked for the Simmons Co. Wrong number - said, is this (something) 7778.
	11:28A	Made another call - no answer.
	11:45A	Sullivan, D.A.'s office on duty
	1:20P	Phone rings - unable to hear conversation. Can hear talking in background.
	1:30P	Phone rings 4 times - hear no conversation.
	1:40P	Can hear some men talking in background.
	1:48P	Phone rings - sounds muffled - rang one - record no conversation.
	2:00P	Someone walking around. Maybe Hodel.
	3:20P	Phone rings 4 times - No answer.
	4:00P	Hronek, D.A.'s office - on duty

HODEL FILE - 45

45

<u>Spool
Time</u>

	4:30P	No movements
	5:00P	No movements
	5:30P	No movements
	6:00P	No movements
	6:19P	Phone rings 7 times. No answer.
	6:30P	No movements
	7:00P	No movements
	7:01P	Phone rang 10 times - no answer
	7:17P	Phone rang 10 times - no answer
	7:30P	No movements
	7:51P	Phone rang 9 times - no answer
	8:00P	No movements
	8:00 PM	All Quiet <u>Meyer, L.A.P.D., on duty</u>
	8:22P	Phone rings 6 times - no answer
	9:00P	All Quiet

9:17P Sounds like Hodel and someone returns home. Hodel says he has a lot of work to do - moving around.

6-11½ 9:20P Hodel and woman talking and moving - woman talking about a skirt - Hodel says, leave it here
Girl - "Have to use bath room - (and she did to)

11½-13 9:35P Hodel and Ellen talking quite low - unable to understand sounds as though Ellen is crying.

13-13½ 9:47P Phone rings - Hodel answers - will try to make it over later - it will be a latish party wont it? Will look at it from a distance, yes, later. Good bye - then Hodel dials phone, but no answer.

10:05P All quiet - sounds as though Hodel is reading or going over papers of some kind.

HODEL FILE - 46   46

Spool
Time

13½-14½ 10:19P   Hodel dials phone - Hello, I just got back to town,
                      hate to bother you so late, do you have report for
                      me? 224, yes, yes, thank you very much. Hodel then
                      uses typewriter.

        10:30P   Hodel moving around house.
        11:09P   Hodel moving around house.
        11:15P   Ellen turns radio on. Hodel asks, can't you do any
                      better than that? Quiet ----
        11:30P   Hodel dials phone - no answer - uses typewriter.
        11:35P   Hodel turns radio up not too loud - Are you tired.
                      Ellen-"no" Hodel sounded as though he said he was
FEB. 26, 1950   going to start packing.
14½-20 12:01A   Phone rings, Hodel answers - "Yes, Harry, how is par
                      asks about party, says he had people over - asks if
                      one o'clock is too late - talks to "Baby Doll" about
                      party. says he will be over. Hodel tells Ellen he
                      is going out to stay up and leave Coline (See news
                      article in Times 2-27-50, page 13, Part I)
                      in. I want to talk to him, will be back in an hour
                      or so. Oh hell, they are all "baby dolls" to me.
                      Uses typewriter again.
        12:13R   Hodel -"Leave Coline in tell him to wait here for me
                      Goes out.
20-21   1:00A   Phone rings - Ellen answers - he isn't here now.
                      Call back in 1½ hrs. will be here in morning.
        1:30A   All quiet.
                      LEWIS ON DUTY, L.A.P.D.

HODEL FILE - 47   47

Spool
Time

21-22	2:00A	Phone rang - maid answered, said Mr. Coline is not in. Repeated 3 times. I don't know (sound as if she was talking to Mr. Hodel) "As he had told her he was expecting Mr. Coline when he left house.
22-23.5	2:40A	Talking by Hodel and maid - Hodel says, I am very ti I am going to sleep, and you had better go to bed to No. No, I am very tired, I am going to sleep.
	2:45A	Radio is now playing soft music.
	3:26A	Radio - turned off. Everything quiet.
	4:00A	Hodel sleeping and snoring.
	6:45A	Still quiet - no sounds.
	7:45A	Lewis Off duty
		B.H. Dreebin - D.A.'s office on duty.
23	8:30A	Hodel snoring very loudly - no other movements.
	9:40A	Hodel moving around - seems to be awake.
	10:00A	no movements
23.5-24	10:40A	Telephone rings - awakened Hodel - said "I'll call you back". Answered by brunting - also "Yes, I'll be there".
24-25	11:35A	Telephone - answering "Yes, yes", mentioned "Carls" Said "I'll get it" apparently went back to sleep.
	12:00noon	Dreebin off duty.

HODEL FILE - 48   48

	12:00noon	Cuncino, D.A.'s office on duty
	12:15P	Hodel coughed loudly - turned radio on to concert program - New York Symphony orchestra. KNX
25-37½	12:30P	Toilet flushes. Water faucet is turned on. Concert music makes Hodel's movements difficult to discern. Sounds like he's shaving now. Completes toilet at approx. 12:40.
	12:45P	Girl enters. Hodel calls her "Helen, of "Ellen" and asks her to take (something) out of the room. She returns. Conversation concerns the music (Beethoven's) Hodel asks for more tea.
	1:00P	Phone rings - Ellen tells Hodel it is Dr. C---- calling. Hodel answers "Yes. Right About what time I'll see you there. Right. Good bye".
	1:30P	Hodel dials phone number - gets busy signal. Turns radio off.
	2:05P	Hodel dials number - gets busy signal. Conversation Hodel asks girl whether she likes the smell. Girl replies "No". Sounds like he's reading newspap
	2:15P	Hodel dials - gets Miss Montgomery Tells her the xx artist is moving out by end of March. (Recorded) Ends conversation with series of yesses. OLympic 3476 is an unlisted number he gave Miss Montgomery. ended 2:40P
	2:45P	Is apparently talking to maid. Difficutl to understand conversation. Tells her to count his woolen sox.

HODEL FILE * 49   49

<u>Spool</u>
<u>Time</u>

	3:00P	Seems to be working in a room alone. Mumbles to himself. Sounds of running water, glasses tinkling, small motor is turned on and off at **intervals**. Off at 4 PM.
1	<u>4:00PM</u>	<u>Hronek, D.A.'s office on duty</u>
37½		Hodel moving around the house.
	4:12P	Hodel taking a bath, splashing and humming to himself.
	4:30P	Movements around the house.
	5:00P	Movements around the house and starts typing.
37½-40	5:26P	Hodel dials the post office - wants to know if there is a letter pickup today at Hwd. & Western Post offi
	5:30P	Hodel instructed Ellen to take it out (the letter) and moving around.
40-42	5:53P	Ellen returns - tells Hodel mail goes out-one at 6:30, one at 9:30, (recorded) Sends her to Wilcox Post Office
42-43	6:52P	Hodel dials Operator, asks for SU 33419 - This is OL 3476. Is Harry there. Call NO 27464.
	7:00P	Hodel moving around the house.
43-44	7:26P	Ellen entered - Hodel apologized for being rude and told her he is expecting some important people 7:30 or 8:00 PM - now let's have some dinner.
44-46½	7:40P	Phone rings - Hodel answers - recorded.
46½-47	7:55P	Phone rings - Hodel answers - "Yea, I'll be right out
	8:10P	Hodel returns.
		<u>HRONEK OFF DUTY</u>

HODEL FILE - 50

50

	8:00P	Crowley, LAPD, on duty
	8:12P	Maid says "hear are the matches".
	8:20P	Maid, "Isn't that away--How miserable I was. Hodel answers - unable to hear, Maid "Did you have a good lunch". Hodel-"Fried eggs, and ---- These are check slips.
47-60	8:23P	Hodel talking to some man. Man "I made six programs you can try out. Talking about germicides and quantities grams 10/1000 etc. Hodel-"what is the effect of 1/10000? Let's go ahead and run our tests Man-"it will take about 50 days to do that". Hodel-"Oranic material that a small percentage of the people are allergic to". Man-We won't mention that" Hodel-"And these are used for restaurant sanitation? Man-"no as for douches, clothing, etc." Hodel-"Well, how do I get it. How much per lb is-----". Man-"35¢ per lb. I think it is//---". Hodel-And the other detergent that you use?" Man-(unable to hear) (recorded)
	8:35P	End of Spool #18 during conversation.
	8:37P	Unable to get much of conversation except talking about detergents. Hodel is very much interested and getting the names of all the manufacturers. Hodel-"what are these detergents normally used for". Man-washing, car shampoos? Hodel-"Is there any dang of them conflicting with the other barbitrates?" Lady-"I could take a bath". Man-"what are you so interested in taking a bath for? "Hodel-would you like a drink"? Man-no thanks.

HODEL FILE - 51   51

	8:44P	Hodel-"Let's build a fire-I'll get some wood". Leaves.
	8:45P	Installed Spool #19
	8:45P	Man-"Do you want the first". Hodel-"No,"sounds of breaking wood. Hodel-"You don't know of any othe possibilities or the key answers"?

SPOOL #19

0-60	8:50P	Hodel-of course you get much more lasting effects from the bath. (Something about 27¢ lb detergent wholesale) Man-but when you take a mixture like "Tide" which is a mixture of ----, and cost per lb of the ingredients. Man-when you consider the millions of packages they sell it not too much. (apparently the man is a chemist who has been doing and synthetics research work in detergents/for Hodel.)
16	9:05P	Man-most of the perfume they have in this stuff is-- Lady-what was that dish with mushrooms in it--- It was on the Blvd. and it wasn't very far. Hodel- I don't remember". Lady-If he didn't have legal representation, he wouldn't even be a Doctor. Hodel-I don't think I have to worry anyway, at least not this year". Lady-"It's necessary to protect you "Career" Hodel-in other words----? Lady----- Hodel-Any felony periods. Lady-bookmaking doesn't count? Lady-How about moral turpitende. Hodel- something about medical profession. Something about tea. Lady-George, you know how I talk to Joe and you weren't home Saturday. I said to Joe, your

24   fried in the "booby batch" He said she not so bad.
I said, how do you know. Lady-you don't go to
Camarillos unless your dangerous to others. Hodel-
or yourself. (Something about alcoholics) Lady-
Oh goody--I'm going to get a bath after all. I smell
awfully now.

9:15P   Lady-we should have brought towels along.

9:20P   Water running in bathroom, and lady says something
about bath tub.

9;25P   Hodel-Thats almost as good as? in this tub. Lady-
I'll take a bath in it. Man-no you won't.
Lady-the only reason I came along was to take a bath.
Man-you wouldn't want to take a bath in an
experimental deal. Hodel-It might eat all your skin
off. Lady-I wouldn't worry with a doctor around.

9:30P   Hodel-wisecracks. Hodel-a peculiar people, the
Persians, the country produces no virgins. They xixic
xllx fuck all day in a violent way, and at night
they practice sexual perversion.

45 9:30P Hodel-these walls are so thin.

9:33P   Water running in bathroom again. Hodel and man
talking about the ingredients (evidently experimenti
with soap in bathroom) Man-what I've seen in your
bathtub and my bathbub-----? mentions sodium sulpha

9:36P   9x36R Telephone rings. Hodel answers - I hope he do
call because the elementary information will be
helpful to me. I'd appreciate any information bedau
I have to make this decision immediately. Thanks
Harry.

HODEL FILE - 53

	9:40P	Hodel-do you want to give me the name of this homicide man. Man-Mr. Morrison.
	9:45P	Hodel-your telephone. Man-OL 4373?
	9:46P	End of Spool #19
	9:47P	Lady talks about making reservations to go to Santa Barbara tomorrow.
	9:50P	Hodel mentions something about murder.
	9:51P	Hodel - place on the strip. Lady mentions Barbara and a japanese place.
	9:52P	Lady-Joe is very friendly toward her. I thought he'd be very unfriendly became-----Hodel-Joe is a little"punchy" you know. How much does it cost to Santa Barbara. She'll get in about 6:00. Lady-It would be so much nicer to go by car , then we could go straight to Court house.
	9:55P	Put on Spool #20
0-3	10:00P	All quiet - all leave for approx. 5 minutes.
3-38	10:05P	Conversation again with same lady and man. Something about having made call. Alimony for her. Lady-I don't want to get involved, I know the poor man will have to pay the cleaning bill.
	10:09P	Telephone rings - (Hear no telephone conversation)
	10:15P	Talking about tea 40¢ or 50 lb. Hodel-the difference between green tea and black tea is------.
	10:17P	Lady-If we go to Santa Barbara, are we going to see Usher? Hodel-He opened up in the county. He's a C.P.A. --- Hodel-something about probation.

	10:20P	Telephone rings twice. Hodel-hello, yes I'm home, just fine, Mr. Sheldon. Very good, anything new with you? I'll give you a ring next week. Have you bought a car yet? (Lady whispering something about Joe and Mexico) Hodel-I have some people here, I'll
	10:25P	call you tomorrow. Hodel-She's subject to deportation However, they'll waver the fact about the papers. Hodel-I don't know where she'd go. Lady-Are you planning on leaving here by any chance. Lady- Did she ever mention it to Bob Adams. Lady- ~~Did xxxxxx xxxxxxx xxxxxx xxxxxxx xxxx xxxxxxxxxx~~ Did Bob say he would (continuous conversation. Able to pick up only bits) All recorded.

ALL

RE-

COR-

DED

	10:30P	Talking about insuring something, value $76,000. If you went to sell it you would get $750.00 Trinkets. Hodel-Had it insured for $104,000. Alimony payments $300 month. Getting it reduced.
	10:35P	Hodel-She looks sick - Lady-Why aren't you selling it, all over the country. Man-Says something "Could not hear" Lady-Well, you'd have to make up
38	10:38P	your mind if want to go. Will you pay 10.00 for a Hodel-I can get a car. Lady-Then, you dont have to worry.
	10:40P	Lady and man left house. (This lady seems to know an awfully lot about the legality of matters, possibly an attorney) End of recording conversation.
	10:44P	Movements in house.
	10:55P	Hodel typing.

HODEL FILE - 55   55

Spool
Time

	10:57P	Hodel arguing with Ellen - unable to understand. Hodel-I didn't think you'd want to talk to her in front of her husband. Ellen-I'm no more than a dishwasher to you. Hodel-I'm sorry.
	11:30P	Noises in the distant part of house.
	11:31P	Hodel-I'm adding Maid ?------Hodel-a little later.
	11:45P	Hodel-working at desk.
	11:55P	Hodel-That's right. I don't car to ~~mixivexitxxxy~~ discuss it any further with you. Take it up with the immigration. Maid talking (unable to hear) Hodel-Was anybody else there. What do you think of me. Hodel typing.

FEBRUARY 27, 1950
	12:00A	Door bell rings. Ellen goes to door. Hodel say - Co in. Turns radio on. Hodel-Did you have a pleasant time in Palm Springs. Unable to hear other parties answer. Radio loud. Mentions "Chicoski".
	12:10A	Hodel - You made the headlines today or tomorrow.
38-40	12:10A	Man-1 made the headlines?
	12:11A	Hodel-Like Hitler said.
40	12:11A	Hodel-your a rich man. Hodel-I can see you beating her up. Woman - Don't bother me. You can't bother me. Man-"(Laughing) Suspicion. Hah. In one place I am a composer of poetry or opera, a hot tempered erratic woman - We've got to get out of here and get some fun for a change.

HODEL FILE - 56

<u>Spool</u>
<u>Time</u>

54-60 12:25A   Hodel-Well anyway, she hasn't said she'd committed
                  incest or killed the Black Dahlia. (other man has
                  an accent - talking about this country) Man-
                  "She said look what you've put in the paper. I hate
                  you." Man-"I've been chased around so much."
                  Hodel-"Whose your Doctor". Man-"On Vine Street.
                  Hodel-"What was the date of your premarital ----.
                  When was your treatment started? When are you going
                  to see him next.
                  End of Spool #20.

        12:30A   Something about 8 units. Hodel-you may be tapering
                  off. Mentioned 4 units.

SPOOL #21

0-27   12:35A   Hodel-"It wouldn't do any harm to wait another month.
                  There are other type of penecillin you are more apt
                  to get the rash on the second----". Man-"
                  She was Queen of Burbank. I'm warning you because
                  I've known you 4 years" (Cannot hear most of con-
                  versation).

10   12:45A   Hodel-Would she ride the girls and make them work?
                  How do you spell it". Man-"LACOA. I'll tell you the
                  whole story. About a year ago ---- 4 girls-they
                  live across from the Catholic church on Argyle. I ha

20   12:50A   a troup , actor Hals; XXXO. .....". Hodel-
                  Right now in Mexico City the value of the collar
                  in pesos. Secretarys work for ---- pesos.

HODEL FILE - 57   57

12:50A $500 will buy? pesos. Hodel-"You don't think
              that the girls try their ----- (Juvenile officers
              observed a 41 cream 4 door Buick parked in front
              of Hodel's residence at this time. license
              #7S1014 registered to Etoyle E. Bennett-Legal
              owner-Hollywood Citizen News).

1:05A   Man-"A girl called named "Ceva" wanted to know about
              (See Times article, page 13, 2-27-50)
              "Rence". Hodel-"You and the girls do solo numbers to
              Man-"Acrobatic numbers, dances, etc." Hodel-"Some-
              thing about a streamlined pussy". Man-Those girls
              are French, they love to travel. I asked one girl
              and she said of course. Coleen or Colee. Hodel-
              "They are all unmarried, aren't they?" Man-"Yes".

27-48   Hodel-"The legal matters are minor. They can get
              married at 18. I would merely be the backers represe
              tative. It would look better.

1:14A   Man-"This is a crucial time for both of us. I told
              "Renee" several times she is the center of all my hope
              Hodel-"We'll really have to ride herd on them. 4 young
              chicks ax in a strange country. Man-"Ha - 4 girls
              and we two. - what a combination. I will be the
              musical director. Someone mentions Dr "Colee".
              Hodel-"I had a friend named Prince ---- who ----
              Hodel-"I'm the only person who knows where all these

48   1:30A   things fit into the picture.

      1:32A   All quiet except for radio.

      1:35A   Hodel-"You better take a generous supply of penecilli
              (Talking to same party)

HODEL FILE - 58
FEBRUARY 27, 1950

48-52	1:45A	All quiet except for radio and someone moving around.
	1:57A	Typing;
		Brechel, LAPD on duty
	2:00A	Typing - radio playing - working at desk.
	4:05A	Turned off radio.
52-55	4:07A	Hodel tells Ellen to go to bed, she has to get up early as they have a lot of things to do, but he wants to sleep late. He tells about getting a lot of work done tonight. She says she won't sleep good.
off		She is nervous.
55-56.5	4:13A	He tells her, come on lets go to bed. They discuss turning on heater.
56.5-61.5	4:15A	Discuss having socks in morning. They talk of his having a cold. She is helping him to undress. She wants some love tonight, but he refuses her. He wants
off		to sleep alone.
	4:22A	Hodel tells Ellen not to argue with him while Dorothy is around. Tells her how to act in company of Dorothy as Ellen then goes to her room, she appears to be angry with Hodel because he sent her to her room without allowing to have any love.
	4:30A	Change spools - put #22 on.
		Hodel retires - alls quiet.

59

HODEL FILE - 59
SPOOL #22 - FEBRUARY 27, 1950

Spool
Time

	8:00A	J. McGrath, D.A.'s office on duty
	9:03A	Phone rings 7 times, no answer. Hodel snoring.
	9:12A	Phone rings 8 times, no answer.
	9:15A	Ellen goes into Hodel's room, wakes him up.
	9:18A	Phone rings 3 times (if answered was in a rear room could not hear)
	11;12A	Phone rings, 12 times, Hodel finally answers but could not make out what was said.
	11:40A	Hodel at desk - typing.

FEBRUARY 27, 1950

	12:00noon	Sullivan D.A.'s office on duty
0-2½	12:10P	Hodel dials and then flushes toilet (recorded) but barely intelligible due to water running-talks about taxes.
2½-3	12:15P	Phone rings - Hodel answers (recorded)
3-3½	12:32P	Phone rings - Hodel answers, "Yes" - (recorded) write to them in Washington".
3½-4½	12:45P	Water running.
	12:50P	Hodel dials phone "Is Mr ? there? (recorded) Will he be in soon? This is Dr. Hodel speaking." Something about account being worked out.
4½-5	12:52P	Hodel dials phone "Is Mr. Neet there? Dr. Hodel speakii Will you be around this afternoon?"
5-6	12:55P	Talking to maid - Cannot make out conversation (recorde(
6-8	1:00P	Hodel dials phone (recorded) No one answers-finally hangs up.
8-13	1:12P	Phone rings - Hodel answers "Oh yes, Al" (recorded)

HODEL FILE - 60

Spool
Time

	1:12P	"Series of yeses agreeing with party on other end. "That sounds pretty good. Wonderful, and his name is Morrison?"
13-14	1:40P	Phone rings - Hodel answered (recorded) "Unable to make a cash outlay at this time".
14-15	2:05P	Hodel dials phone (recorded) "I have some business in Detroit for a few days".
15-15½	2:38P	Hodel dials phone (recorded)
	2:45P	Hodel typing.
	3:15P	Quiet since 3 PM. Hodel apparently out of house.
	3:59P	Still quiet.
	4:00P	Hronek, D.A.'s office on duty.
	4:22P	Phone rings - 16 times, no answer
	4:27P	Phone rings 7 times, no answer.
	4:52P	Phone rings 5 times, no answer.
	5:00P	All Quiet.
	5:30P	All quiet.
	6:00P	All quiet.
	6:12P	Phone rings 10 times, no answer.
15-17	6:20P	Someone named Joe used the phone, hear him moving around (Recorded)
17-18	6:45P	Someone with German accent talked with Ellen - hard to understand.
18-20	6:51P	Ellen talking to someone about something.
	7:00P	All quiet.
	7:30P	All quiet.
	8:00P	All quiet - Off Duty.

HODEL FILE - 61   61

Spool
Time

	8:00P	Bimson, LAPD on duty
	8:20P	Someone enters - no conversation - typing.
20-34	8:35P	Typing very fast - strange shuffling noises unable to identify - recording conversation believe it's between Hodel and Joe. Mostly unintelligible. Hodel says there is a possibility of a place near Washington and Normandy.
	8:45P	Mentions Finlays - says somebody started from San Francisco, should be here in a couple of days. Talking about some woman, says she needs cheering up, Hodel say I'll be going up past Santa Barbara and if you want a lift to Camarillo and back I'll drop you off and pick you up a couple of hours later.
	9:30P	Maid entered - short conversation - unable to understand.
34-38	9:40P	Scuffling noise and conversation between a man and woman - unable to understand.
38-55	11:10P	Conversation between Hodel and Ellen - Hodel asks her what she plans to do if he manages to raise some money says she has several alternatives - they are arguing Sounds of dishes and eating - Hodel tells her she can collect $10. per week social security for 26 weeks - tells her if any lady asks to tell them she has only been getting $50. per mo. instead of $100. to avoid income tax. Sounds like Ellen is crying. Hodel is explaining how she can beat tax - sounds like she is on her way out soon.

End of
Spool

HODEL FILE - 62
SPOOL #23
Spool
Time

	11:30P	Install Spool #23
0-3	11:45P	Sends night letter to George Hodel - 249 So. Harvard.
		night letter sounds like double talk.
3-33	11:52P	Company arrives-Hodel says "come in Theodore "

talking about a woman by the name of Renee. Theodore
says all this woman can talk about is how much she love:
him. Sounds very theatrical. Talk about $10,000.
and why he married her. He repeats time and again that
she said "This is a trap". Talking of attorneys. Then
reads Hodel what sounds like a divorce paper. Hodel an
friend talking and laughing at Courts and legal procedu
Sounds as if Hodel is putting Theodore up for night.
Turns on radio - resumes typing.

FEB. 28, 1950

	1:40A	xirks Hodel says to Ellen "Why do you have your coat on?
		I'm buring up in here". Can't hear Ellen answer.
33-	1:55A	Conversation between Hodel and Ellen, sounds like
60		writing on desk. Ellen says "How will they treat me".
		Brechel, LAPD relieves Bimson
		Hodel quotes prices of tea. He speaks Spanish with Ell
		Hodel recites poetry.
	2:20A	Turns radio off. Walks around. Checks doors. Goes
off		to lavatory.
	2:35A	Hodel and Ellen in bedroom - not much conversation
0-13		mostly whispered. Sounds indicate both in bed,
		probably making love.
	2:50A	Sounds indicate Hodel reading in bed.
	3:30A	Hodel snoring.

HODEL FILE - 63

63

FEBRUARY 28, 1950

Spool #23

	8:00A	Morgan relieves Brechel
13-16	8:20A	Telephone rang - Hodel "I've been working pretty hard father", etc. - "Do you know when these people will be there for the furniture?" etc. - ends - "OK Dad fine, goodbye".
	9:25A	Typing
16-17	9:30A	Hodel (on telephone) unintelligible conversation about rates - ends "Thank you".
17-19	9:35A	Hodel (On telephone) "Uh-huh - I'll appreciate it, otherwise I'd have to buy more blankets you see, et I phoned you for the last six or eight weeks - etc. Ends "Alright thank you, goodbye".
19-218X4 21½	9:45A	Hodel (On telephone) "Pretty good, thank you" etc. Maybe we could finish - etc. When would be a con- venient time for you? Thursday I may be going to Santa Barbara - I have things pretty well worked ou already - I'll have to make a breakdown on expenses etc. I have that all tabulated - we could sit down an hour and work it out - etc. Ends - "Alright fin Very good, goodbye".
21½- 21 3/4	9:55A	Telephone rang - Hodel - "yes, etc. You just want one pound - ends "Alright, goodbye".
	10:08A	Typing
21 3/4- 22½	10:10A	Desk noise
22½- 23½	10:42A	Hodel - conversation with Ellen - unintelligible.

HODEL FILE - 64		64
	10:45A	Airplane noise
23½-24	10:50A	Unintelligible conversation - Hodel and Ellen
24-24½	10:55A	Unintelligible conversation - Hodel and Ellen
24½-25	11:05A	Telephone rang - no answer
25-27½	11:12A	Telephone rang - no answer
	11:13A	Ellen - "Your phone rang" - Hodel - "Find out who it is" Ellen-"Just a moment - Jimmy?" Hodel-what's the name?" Ellen-"It's Jimy (something)" Hodel-"Tell him, I'll be with you in just a minute. Just leave it there". Toilet noise - Hodel (unintelligible conversation) ends. "Yes-Goodbye".
27½-27 3/4	11:30A	Telephone rang - Hodel - "Hello, yes, between 10:30 and 11:00? Does she know where to meet him? I'll tell him - bye".
27 3/4-28	11:35A	Hodel - (on telephone) "Will he be in tonight? I'll call him".
28-28¼	11:55A	Telephone rang - Hodel "hello, no we don't need any help now, your welcome".
	12:00	Hodel in bathroom - filled tub.
	12:00noon	Bill Snyder relieves Morgan
28¼-29	12:30P	Phone rings - (recorded) Not much xxxxxxxxxixnxxith
29-29½	12:35P	Conversation with Ellen - (recorded)
29½-30½	1:00P	Hodel talking to Ellen - (recorded) unintelligible Hodel climbed up or down some stairs - sounds of digging or something similar.
30½-31½	1:05P	Hodel talking to Ellen - asks for blanket or something (recorded)
31½-32	1:10P	Hodel continues talking to Ellen (recorded)

Hodel File - 65 ⁶⁵

	1:30P	Sounds of pounding or hammering - Hodel has few wor with Ellen. Unintelligible - flushes toilet and breaks wind at same time. Ye Gods - what a racket (not recorded)
32-33	1:40P	Phone rings - Hodel answers - (recorded) states someone is coming to see house.
33-33½	1:50P	Phone rings - Hodel answers - very short (recorded)
	2:15P	Plenty of noise from passing cars and trucks.
	2:20P	Hodel dials phone twice - no answer. Continued hammering and pounding (not recorded)
33½-34½	2:25P	Phone rings - Hodel answers - so much noise from outside could not understand (recorded)
	2:35P	Hodel talking to himself, but hardly above a whisper
	3:00P	Hodel does a bit of typing - no talk - not recorded
34½-35	3:15P	Hodel dials phone - recorded
35-46	3:35P	Hodel talks to someone in regards to house - (this party is female) also talke about Chinese art (recorded) conversation faded out due to Hodel and party going to some other part of house.
	4:00P	Snyder over to ~~Phillxix~~ McGrath, D.A.'s office
	4:02P	Phone rang 8 times, no answer
46-48	4:10P	Phone call - not able to understand all parts - said he & Mrs Hodel divorced - also something about children - Hodel became very angry, said "I do not like your questiong-is none of your business. I do not desire to deal with you." Hodel hung up phone (recorded)
	4:13P	Hodel typing.

HODEL FILE - 66   66

48-55	5:06P	Phone call (recorded) could not understand (lots of noise and static.) Sounds like trouble in receiving set - said something about 75¢ a hour als see you 12 to 6 - come on out and try it.

Spool #24

	5:40P	Changed to Spool 24
0-1.5	5:40P	Funny sounding noises (recorded) for a couple of minutes.
	5:45P	Typing
1.5-4	5:46P	More funny noises (recorded)
4-7	5:47P	Phone rings (recorded) Hodel answers "Hello dear. Things are very much status quo". Conversation som what unintelligible due to noises in background. "Well definitely try to see you this week-end. Dorero. (his ex-wife)
	5:55P	Funny noises continue since telephone conversation then some typing.
	6:10P	Lt. Frank Jaminson phoned, said Hodel moving furnit out - if Bug is found or all furniture moved phone him at CR 14917. His name is pronounced (JAMINSON) any time, day or night.
7-23	6:50P	Hodel in conversation - could not make out too much noise. May have been on phone - (tried at 6:53 to record some of the conversation). "Expense along that line - tell you where I see you - what date wil this be "Sat". right, shall I come alone or bring another girl - do you have enought? Also talked ab going somewhere Sat. 2 blks So. of Colorado, 6 Bl. E of Verdugo - the West end of Eagle Rock "I'll just call her Jill" Have you met some of my friends - se

67

HODEL FILE - 67

	6:50P	you Saturday how are you fixed for girls? I'm too old now - it does not make any difference to me now Did you decide to take the other room? (It seems th person may be renting or buying the house.)
	8:00P	Bimson, LAPD, on duty.
	8:10P	Hodel moving around - no conversation
	9:30P	Hodel enters - heavy rasping noise lasts approx. 30 minutes, can't identify - no conversation-heavy breathing.
	10:20P	Someone writing at desk.
23-54	11:40P	Conversation - talk about selling something for $60 Sounds like a car - conversation very low. Lots of interference - talking about art - believe Hodel is talking to Chris. Talking about houses and somethi about Monday the 6th. Hodel says he needs $16,000. says there is $15,000. against his house.
54-54½	1:20P	Hodel makes phone call - asks if he should come bac now or in the morning.
	1:25P	Hodel typing - company gone.
Spool 25	1:30P	Change spool - put on #25 Brechel, LAPD on duty.
	2:00A	Hodel working around. No conversation.
	2:50A	Hodel retires. Snoring. Have not heard Ellen talk since on duty.

68

HODEL FILE - 68

March 1, 1950
SPOOL #25
Spool
Time   8:00A   Morgan relieves Brechel

0-1   9:10A   Hodel(Telephoned) "She can come over about one - hav
                           her call me - ends "Alright thank you, goodbye".

1-2   9:27A   Telephone rang - Hodel, "Yes Sir" - conversation abou
                           cold tablets - "Follow directions - I hope it breaks
                           up right away". Ends -"goodbye".

2-2.6   9:35A   Telephone rang - Hodel "Yes, I'll call him, will you
                           wait just a moment pleast - Mr. Phillips would you
                           mind calling the number again, and he'll answer it -
                           I won't answer it you see".

              9:55A   While in bathroom, Hodel said to himself "I wish I
                           hadn't done that" (Probably blew his nose too hard -
                           or something)

2.6-4   10:08A   Telphone rang - Hodel "Hello - etc (water running in
                           tub makes voice unintelligible)

4-6   10:12A   Conversation (with unidentifiable man) Hodel "Are
                           they both looking good?" (Water isn't running during
                           conversation; however, conversation is held out of
                           bathroom and hard to understand) Hodel "I was
                           surprised" "Thanks" (went back to bathroom and turne
                           water back on).

6-7.5   10:24A   Doorbell rang - conversation between Hodel and Ellen
                           (something about breakfast)

7.5-8   10:25A   Hodel and Ellen, very short conversation.

              10:26A   Hodel "He already left" (at front door)

8-12   10:30A   Hodel, "Say Ellen", etc. - conversation about tea -
                           Hodel - "Go where" (Scraping noise)

HODEL FILE - 69

(This spool #25 and following should be checked with
federal income tax man in the future as Hodel's income
tax is computed with this man, and it looks like they
about to "take" Uncle for a few bucks.)

12toend   10:35A   Conversation between Hodel and Ellen (Unintelligible)
doorbell rang - Hodel answers - talking to some man -
Hodel and man enter library - Hodel "Your fault or
mine" - Conversation about radio announcer - man
(probably Mr. Hagan), "She moved to San Francisco".
Conversation about a wealthy man who owned five gasoli
stations - Hodel "Is he a good guy". Hagan, "Yes"
etc., conversation about auction-something about FBI
Hodel "I had an offer in Hawaii" - conversation about
tea (men sat down at desk - everything clearly recorde
hereon) Conversation about making out Hodel's income
tax - conversation about Mrs. Hodel, alimony, support
children - conversation about exemptions - conversatio
about inventory - about chinese international export
company - about corportations - about five hundred
dollar debt owed Hodel - about corporation books -
about Hodel's books - Hagan "We have no choice in the
matter", etc. Hodel asked operator for Atlantic 66403
Hodel "Well alright, will you ask him to call me pleas
No, this is Doctor Hodel" (End) Men check figures
(Hagan reads and Hodel checks) conversation about
total income-about asking for money back - Hodel -
"You accountants and auditors sure make things complicated". Hagan, "No, we don't" etc. - about stock.

HODEL FILE - 70

	11:20A	Telephone rang - Hodel, "Hello", etc (unintelligible because of loud filing noise) Conversation with Hagan about goodwill being capital gain (long pause) conversation continues about stock - about "Showing it as an advance".
SPOOL 26	11:22A	Wire changed to Spool #26
	11:30A	Morgan requested Bimson to check cars parked in front of Hodel residence.
O-end	11:32A	Hagan, "people call me Mr. Gahagan" - laughter - conversation about income tax. Hagan "Are you married now"? Hodel-"No".
	12:00	Walter Sullivan relieves Morgan
	12:01P	Telephone rang - very short conversation
	12:10P	(Bimson reports that there were two cars parked in front of Hodel's #1 - 51R392, a '47 Pontiac Convertab Sedan, registered to Floyd Hagan - 3208 Montezuma Ave. Alhambra. #2 - 9P3 938, a '47 Chevrolet Coupe, registered to Willie Wheeler, 4461 Town Ave., L.A.)
	12:05P	Hodel still in conversation with his acct. (being recorded) (Spools 25 and 26 and 27 will prove very interesting to income tax investigators)
	12:10P	Phone rings - Hodel answers "Yes, whose calling". Conversation regarding house (sale).
	12:12P	HO 93311 - (This conversation may be OK on recorder)
	12:17P	Phone rings. Hodel answers (recorded)
	12:35P	Discussing and checking figures with acct.
	12:45P	Hodel reading off figures and acct. either putting the in adding machine or typewriterx.

HODEL FILE - 71   ⁷¹

	12:50P	Changing to Spool #27 - Hodel still reading off figures.
<u>Spool 27</u>	12:55P	Started Spool 27. Still with acct. Tabulating figures.
O-22	1:10P	Recorder stops for about 1 min. Found tiny piece of wire which seemed to be shorting recorder.
	1:11P	Working OK now.
	1:15P	Trouble on recorder. Intermittent slipping - called crime lab. and reported to Stanton.
	1:17P	Recorder off. Airplane noise. No further conversatio Apparently account left premises while recorder was giving us trouble.
22-23½	1:25P	Some conversation (recorded) Could not distinguish voices.
23½-24	1:27P	More conversation. Believe with acct. (being recorded
24-28½	1:30P	Conversation (recorded) on figures.
	1:35P	Recorder stops at about 28½
29-33½	1:36P	Started recorder again. After moving reel forward.
	1:37P	Phone rings. Hodel answers "I don't know. Unable to refer you to anyone". Much noise in background.
~~33½~~	1:38P	Phone rings, No conversation. Continues talking to acct.
	1:39P	Recorder stops again at 33½
35-36	1:45P	Started recorder again. Still jumping.
	1:46P	Tabulating figures, lots of noise.
	1:55P	Sullivan called to telphone.
		By Morgan-Recorder on the blink - further tax computa- tions are discussed between Hodel and Hagan.

HODEL FILE - 72   72

	2:00P	Telephone rang - Hodel "Helo, just a moment". Telephone apparently for Hagan - Hagan "Been busy uh-huh". Conversation related to income tax problem made date for Tuesday at 4:30 o'clock - at 35 North Arroyo (not recorded) Conversation ended 2:04 PM.
	2:05P	Hodel telephoned "Hello Deak". "Albert Band who was John Huston's assistant called you this morning - call him at Hollywood 93311 - He asked for Dorothy". End 2:07P
37-39½	2:10P	Turned on recorder at 37. Still discussing income ta with acct.
to	2:11P	Phone rings. Hodel answers (recorder still working. Stops at 39½ but starts again). Unable to get any
	2:13P	of phone conversation. Recorder stop at 41. Starts again. Recorder starts and stops.
51	2:20P	"I don't want to specify. I don't want to call it to their attention that such things are going on". (Acct. makes above statement).
	2:21P	Phone rings. Hodel answers.
	2:25P	Spool runs out reading 51.

Spool #28

0-8	2:26P	Conversation between Hodel and acct.
	2:30P	Start spool #28. (Started recording).
0-3	2:30P	"Ok, George, will see you later". Hodel-"How much will this cost? Good bye."
3-4	2:41P	Conversation with Ellen (recorded) unintelligible.
	3:15P	Telephone rings answered by Hodel - said, "Hello, I'll be down right away".
	3:25P	Radio is turned on

HODEL FILE - 73

	3:30P	Radio off.
4½-5	3:35P	Conversation with Ellen.
	3:45P	Phone rings. Hodel answers. "He's already left". (Apparently refers to accountant).
	3:46P	Phone rings. Hodel answers "He just left, I'll see if I can get him". No further.
5-7	3:48P	Conversation with Ellen. (recorded) Noise in background.
7-7½	4:00P	Conversation with Ellen (recorded).
	4:00P	Frank Hronek, D.A.'s office on duty.
7½-10	4:10P	Conversation with Ellen. Much racket. (recorded).
10-22	4:27P	Hodel invites some lady in, discussing the house and furniture - sounds like a couple of women.
22-26	4:45P	Returned from examination of different rooms and furth discussion.
26-29	4:53P	Hodel talks with Ellen.
	4:59P	Hodel starts typing.
29-33	5:32P	Hodel talking with a man.
	6:00P	Moving around and typing.
	6:30P	Typing.
	7:00P	All quiet.
	7:30P	Hodel starts typing again.
	8:00P	Meyer, LAPD, on duty.
33-34½	8:10P	Hodel calls someone on phone - asks where Michigan State College is - East Lansing - Thanks them - hangs up - starts typing.
	8:27P	Hodel phones - "is Slim there. Have him call me when he comes in."

HODEL FILE - 74

Spool
Time

34½-35   8:37P   Ellen enters - asks if can turn radio on - Hodel
                   says, "Sure". Hodel says something about helping
                   Ellen bring in the table. Radio on - Hodel typing.

          9:10P   Hodel still typing.

          9:30P   Hodel around - all quiet.

          10:00P   Hodel around - all quiet.

          10:30P   Hodel around - all quiet.

          11:10P   Hodel dials phone - no answer - still typing1

          11:30P   Phone rang - Hodel answers. Didn't say anything.
                   Ellen turned radio on again.

35-40½   11:37P   Phone rang. Hodel answered - Whoever he was talking
                   he said, "Don't say anything over the phone - it is k
                   tapped - said he had there phone number, and would ca
                   tomorrow - said he would have to go out to call -
                   checked but would not repeat number on phone. Said
                   it is WE 1670 and he knew name of Street. Would
                   have phone people check - said if he said phone numbe
                   "They" would be out and bother them - that is what
                   "They" always do. When Hodel hung up, Ellen asked hi
                   how he knew-Hodel said he was just talking. Still
                   typing.

MAR 2   12:05A   Hodel still typing.

          12:45A   Hodel still typing.

          1:15A   Hodel still typing and talking to Ellen - unable to
                   understand.

          1:45A   Hodel still typing and talking to Ellen - unable to
                   understand.

HODEL FILE - 75   75

Spool
Time

                Brechel, LAPD on duty.

2:00A   Hodel still typing

2:20A   Hodel stops typing. Tells Ellen to put things away
                exactly as she finds them. Hodel goes out. Alls
                quiet except for radio.

2:27A   Hodel returns - goes to desk - resumes typing.

3:45A   Typing - stops - radio turned off.

4:05A   Hodel retires - All is quiet.

HODEL FILE - 76

March 2, 1950

Spool #28

	8:00A	Morgan relieves Brechel
4.5-42	9:10A	Door-bell rang (someone walking)
42-42.2	11:32A	Typing Begins
	11:40A	Hodel, "Ellen, if you get any mail you'll have it without an instants delay".
	12:00 noon	J. McGrath, D.A.'s office on duty
42-43	∄	Someone phoned - Hodel said "are you here now - yes, it just came ½ an hour ago.
	12:07P	Ellen and Hodel talking about some woman. Hodel said, "Tell her to wait, maybe she will leave it at the door.
	12:10P	Door bell rang - Hodel said to Ellen, "Be nice to her, she is an old lady". Hodel still working at his desk.
43-45	12:12P	Hodel makes phone call - (recorded) to a Mr. Overton. Hodel to Mr Overton "I was wondering about RE 4279, it is disconnected".
45-49	12:13P	(Recorded) Hodel makes another phone call - talks abou RE 4279, and WE 6128. Also about some tests of some ki
49-54	12:14P	Hodel phones the Phone company - asked to have NO 27464 disconnected. Had talk with Phone company.
SPOOL 29-12:30P		Spool No. 29 put on
0-1	12:32P	Hodel makes phone call (recorded)
1-3.5	12:34P	Hodel phone call to a Mr. Arnell (recorded) Talked about running something down - a piece of machinery or something.

HODEL FILE - 77   77

	1:15P	Someone comes to the door - talks about 3 keys and phones.
	1:55P	Hodel asks for phone number of Dow Chemical Company.
3.5-15		Hodel phones - asks for Mr. Morrison - talk about chemical for a bath soap. Asks questions regarding various chemicals.
	2:16P	Reception getting bad, also appears Hodel now using pho in rear of house - hard to hear - other phone pulled ou by Telephone Company.
	2:40P	Hodel makes phone call - no response.
	2:41P	Phone rings - Hodel answers - says "Hello" then hangs up and dials - phone rings again. Hodel says "Hello" then hangs up.
15-21	2:42P	Called Dr. Hussey regarding a test of some kind (recorde Also said something regarding CK 15258 - could be a phone CR 15258.
	4:00P	Hodel typing. -(Hronek, D.A.'s office on duty)
21-23	4:07P	Phone rings - Hodel answers.
23-28	4:24P	Hodel dials operator"BR 20666 - OL 3476. Mr. Lock, thi is Dr. Hodel------" Something about microscopes - abou how much do they sell for - suppose you send me some literature - can you get us a reasonable price - about 3:00 or 3:30PM.
	4:32P	Starts typing again.
28-30	4:39P	NO 27464 - Interior Decorator.
30-31	4:49P	Hodel talked with Ellen - walked around.
	5:00P	Starts typing.

HODEL FILE - 78

31-33	5:16P	Phone rings - Hodel answers - saw some notice in the paper - "I have a house which I am willing to rent - one wing anyway - (recorded) "I'll be in and out - suppose you call on me tomorrow or Saturday".
33-34	5:50P	Hodel dials - (recorded) couldn't understand.
34-35	6:12P	Phone rang 8 times. No answer. Hodel apparently out for supper.
	6:30P	All quiet.
	7:00P	All quiet.
	7:30P	All quiet.
	8:00P	All quiet - Hronek off duty.
	8:00P	Meyer, LAPD, on duty
	8:30P	All quiet.
	9:00P	All quiet.
	9:10P	Phone rings 18 times, no one answers.
	9:30P	All quiet
	10:00P	All quiet
	10:30P	All quiet
	10:50P	Sounds as though Hodel and Ellen returned home. Some one moving around.
34-40	11:00P	Hodel calls someone - tells them had other phone disconnected and changes phone from time to time - was on phone 15 min., but didn't say much - asked what happened today and just listened.
	11:30P	Hodel still around, but quiet.
3-3-50	12:00A	All quiet.
	12:30A	Hodel and Ellen moving around, talk a little.
	1:10A	Hodel starts typing.
	1:30A	Hodel still around.

HODEL FILE - 79

MARCH 3, 1950

	1:30A	Brechel, LAPD on duty
	2:00A	All is quiet.
	2:10A	Hodel enters den probably from patio. Obtains somethin; from desk - then leaves room via patio. Hodel probabl; in studio.
	2:30A	Hodel enters lavatory - runs water - urinates - talks to himself "This is too hot". Goes to desk - writes with pen.
	2:40A	Begins typing.
	3:00A	Typing stops - Hodel leaves room.
	3:05A	Hodel returns to den - works at desk.
	3:15A	Hodel leaves room. All is quiet.
	3:20A	Very faint noise of phone ringing 5 times.
	3:25A	Hodel returns to desk in den. Mumbles to himself. Seems to be reading.
	3:40A	Hodel leaves room.
	4:00A	Hodel returns with Ellen - she goes to lavatory. Hodel - "Did it come off alright?" Answer not readabl
40-44.5	4:03A	Hodel speaks Spanish to Ellen. She answers in Spanish She then tells him the words in English. She seems to be coaching him on Spanish. They enter lavatory. Hod says "You didn't come in here to wash your hands dress in that thing". She whispers an answer. He sends her
off		out of room "to avoid hard feelings".
44.5-46	4:10A	Hodel and Ellen have conversation in Spanish. They are in bedroom having sex intercourse or something, probably perversion. Sounds like he got another blow-job.

HODEL FILE - 80

4:30A	Snoring begins. Hodel asleep.
8:20A	Hodel arises, goes to lavatory.
8:25A	Hodel and Ellen talking. Not much conversation. Could not make out.
8:30A	Ellen goes to lavatory.

HODEL FILE - 81

Spool #29

3-3-50,	8:00A	Bimson, LAPD, on duty
	10:00A	Hodel gets up - says "come in Joe" says "There is a not on the phone".
	10:30A	Hodel walking about - washes
	11:00A	Hodel still walking about - muttering to himself
	11:30A	Phone rings - Hodel says "About how soon Mr Kesler" "Very well, I'll be here".
46-47	11:35A	Woman knocks on door, says "George, may I use your bathroom". Hodel says, "Sure come on in". Conversation between this woman and Hodel - they both leave bathroom
47-55		xxxxxxxxxxxxxxxxxxxxxxxxx conversation - phone rin answered by Hodel, says, "That's all right - tomorrow after 11", hangs up - sounds like he is making a medical exam. Hodel leaves - goes into library.
55-65	11:45A	Conversation between Hodel and woman - typing - conversa tion regarding branch library - pounding in background. Conversation regarding a play.
Spool 30-12:00P		Changing reel - Sullivan, D.A.'s office on duty.
	12:00P	Phone rings, Hodel answers, "Let me look and see".
0-6	12:07P	Lady talking (recorded) "I owe 4 times 75.00, that's 300.00 (Possibly his wife) "I have to pay my rent or get out".
	12:15P	Conversation with woman continues. Relative to her expenses and the childrens.

HODEL FILE - 82   82

6-10	12:16P	Conversation continues (recorded)
	12:19P	Quiet.
10-12	12:21P	Conversation with wife resumed (recorded) He talks about a job.
12-24	12:28P	More conversation (recorded) Hodel "I've lost money every year". Talking about what money she's earned. Hodel discusses his lossess "$6000;00 in 1946, "I sold the clinic to pay for the losses of that year. Now, I must sell the house. Hodel-something about pennitentia Noises in background.
	12:40P	Quiet.
	12:41P	Conversation resumed. Much racket Hodel-"I can give yo 2 or 300.00 a month."
24-28	12:42P	Started recording "What would you advise me doing?" Static - hard to understand conversation.
	12:46P	Conversation fades. Apparently parites went to some ot part of house.
	12:50P	Phone rings. Footsteps, but hear no answer.
	12:51P	A man talking to Hodel - "Anxious to get located in thi area. I have my own firm. We sell yadage. Office at 610 S. Broadway. Negotiating for another office on La Cienega". "Bamboo blinds of various kinds".
	12:54P	Conversation fades.
	1:08P	Conversation with unknown man resumes. "I think I'll t the place". Man leaves.
	1:10P	Conversation with woman (wife?)
28-38	1:11P	Started recording. She's talking about the children. "I'm not too happy about Kelvin". Much racket. Hodel talks about having wife and children with him again.

HODEL FILE - 83

	1:21P	Conversation continues. Low tones.
38-48	1:28P	Started recording. Can't make out conversation, but hope recording is getting it. Hodel reading from Mexic paper about jobs in Mexico.
	1:38P	Hodel reading to wife from some sort of manuscript.
48-49	1:40P	Hodel threw reading. resumes conversation.
	1:44P	Dials phone (recorded) Wrong number.
	1:45P	Dials phone-No conversation.
49-50	1:51P	Dials phone - "Is he there? This is Dr. Hodel. You ha n't typed my report yet? Have him call me".
	1:55P	Hodel and wife continue conversation. Talking about ak their income tax. Man arrives "Dr Hodel - We'll be thr here in a few minutes". Man replies, "I'm going back to see Ellen".
	1:56P	Typing.
	2:00P	Working on her income tax.
	2:10P	Wife talking on phone. Sounded like she called party, Carol.
	2:12P	Wife to Hodel - I won't be able to go today. I'll probably see over the weekend". Much racket and typing
50-55	2:17P	(recorded) Conversation between wife and Hodel "She get some cash and hide it somewheres".
	2:24P	Max Much interference in receiving. Man talking to Hod Unable to recognize voice or his conversation very clear
55-61	2:26P	"When I came in at 6 AM, I parked the car. It was all quiet". (recorded)
	2:28P	Phone rings - Hodel answers "Yes, I know who it is". Apparently talking to tax expert. "I'm very anxious to see the flower shop. I'll see you today.

HODEL FILE - 84

2:30P	Resumes conversation with man.
2:31P	Out of recording wire. Crime lab has been notified by Belle.
2:32P	Conversation continues. Man talks about displaying the product to a woman. She finally agreed in about 30 to 60 days she'd put thru a 7 or 7 fifty order. "I had 2 - 6.00 tins, 2 - 12.00 tins, and 12 - 3.75 tins." This man is apparently a tea salesman for Hodel. "Our firm is like the Rolls Royce Firm. It's small but it's the best".
2:49P	Phone rings. Hodel answers. Again discussing his income tax. "Take 101.00 out of the commission. That will save her a few dollars".
2:50P	Salesman again talking. "I had 45.00 to make the trip. If you had sent me the 25.00 sonner, I'd have done a better job. The tires are only good for another 60 day: Blew 2 tires on the trip, one out of Modesto; one out of Fresno. (Lots of bull).
3:20P	Salesman still talking. nothing from Hodel. All about the tough breaks on the trip. "I'm supposed to report to Presidio Monday AM for active duty. I got .21 in my pocket and I got to get back up there. I'll work from 8:30AM to 4:30PM, and will have Saturday and Sunday off I can still handle the tea on weekend trips.
3:25P	This guy has talked continuously since 2:25PM.
3:26P	Phone rings - Hodel answers "Whose calling?" "200 toda: Is that it? Why don't you talk to her about that?" (water running) Can't hear no more.

HODEL FILE - 85

3:28P	Salesman again talking. Talked about selling some ash-trays. "They found my blood-pressure at 160. They gave me some pills. Will you take my blood-pressure". Both men walk away.
3:35P	Quiet.
3:45P	Phone - "I just thought you might know something". Hodel talking to some one. "Radiator 10.00.
3:50P	Phone being dialed. "Is this Mrs. Gomez. This is the China? This is the salesman talking. The little electr stove. We got to get rid of this stuff within the next 24 hrs. Have some ply wood and some lumber. We have 3 windows and odds and ends of lumber. We need the space. Could you call this evening. No matter how late. You can sell this stuff. There is 650.00 worth of merchandi We'll take $110.00 for everything. We don't have time t run an ad. You'll come at 8 o'clock and the boss and I will be waiting for you. 8 o'clock tonight." Hung up and then Hodel and salesman had a good laugh.
4:00P	"We'd better go-to be back here by 8 o'clock, but I want you to take my blood-pressure first". Hodel,"it's 164." "What are these pills". Hodel-"They look like pheno-b.
4:01P	Belle here with more wire.
4:05P	Phone call. Unable to hear conversation due to noise.
4:10P	Hodel- "HO 91234" (salesman dials) Asks about ad in papers of March, Shangarala - unusual studio rooms or apartment in luxurous modernistic home for axits artist writer. $40.00, 90.00, Ph. OL 3476, put it in tomorrow' paper $1.52 Dr. Geo. Hodel.

HODEL FILE - 86
SPOOL 31

	4:20P	Hodel and salesman leave.
	4:23P	Fire Department passes Hodel's home.
	4:24P	Hronek, D.A.'s office on duty
0-2	4:46P	Hodel dials, Mr. Oberley - he can be there in 20-25 min Has a conversation with someone
	5:00P	All quiet
	5:30P	All quiet
	5:50P	Phone rang 2 times, no answer
	6:00P	All quiet
	6:30P	All quiet
	7:00P	All quiet
	7:30P	All quiet
	7:49P	Phone rang 3 times, no answer
	8:00P	All quiet, Hronek off duty
	8:00P	All quiet - Meyer LAPD, on duty
	8:30P	All quiet, sounds as though Ellen is running the vacuum cleaner.
2-3	8:48P	Phone rang, Ellen answered, party must have asked for Hodel. Ellen said he wasn't home yet.
3-4	9:01P	Phone rang, Ellen answered, says she will give Hodel the message. He should be home soon.
4-5	9:07P	Phone rang. Ellen took a message for Hodel. Didn't repeat anything.
	9:10P	Hodel and some man came in - talk in other part of house Vacuum cleaner going - can't hear anything.
5-6	9:15P	Hodel and man talk about arranging something.
6-12	9:23P	Hodel calls "Nickey", and asks her over - says he will m some drinks - bring some girl along, asks her if she wil read some poems - a friend is with him.

HODEL FILE - 87

12-17½	9:26P	Hodel tells man some girls are coming over - one is 26, a legal secretary to some lawyer. Man asks if girl is going along to Santa Barbara. Talk about 3 girls comin over in about 30 minutes.
	9:47P	Hodel trys to phone 3 times, no answer - tells man no one answered.
17½-18	9:50P	Hodel and man talk about a phone number. Hodel said he wasn't sure-repeated number. HO 94142. Wasn't sure about the 2.
18-19	9:52P	Man trys phone - asks for Miss Jackson - says HO 94140 Trys again - says HO 94142 - then repeats 24376-trys another number - no answer.
	10:01P	Radio on
	10:16P	Hodel asks operator number of some theater - then repeats HO 93131. Calls and asks if anyone is at ticket agency desk.
19-21	10:20P	Man asks Hodel about mailing a letter - wanted her to get it tomorrow - Man asks Hodel for a complete physica check-up. Hodel checks man's blood pressure - talks ab that - Hodel tells him he couldn't get insurance.
21-23½	10:30P	Girls arrive - unable to understand - are in another ro Lot of laughing.
	11:00P	Still in another part of house.
	11:13P	Other man comes in. Hodel introduces girls as Nickey-Shirley-Judy. Talking about a deoderizing bath salt, Hodel said he just used.

HODEL FILE - 88   88

	11:45P	Playing some kind of guessing game.
3-4-50	12:15A	Still playing same game
	12:45A	Playing a new guessing game
23½-24½	1:27A	Phone rang, Hodel answered - didn't say anything. Meyer off duty.
	1:30A	G.L.Wean, LAPD, on duty
	1:50A	Playing cards
	2:20A	Playing records, can't hear conversation
	3:30A	Visitors left - Hodel apparently gone to bed.
	8:00A	Morgan relieves Wean
24½-25	9:30A	Telephone rang - no answer
25-32	9:37A	Telephone rang - man in house woke up Hodel. Man-"Telephone, George". Hodel-"Hello" - conversation unintelligible - Hodel went to bathroom - returned to phone - Hodel "I don't know where he is. I'll be here today".
32-33	11:35A	Hodel and Ellen - unintelligible conversation.
33-33½	11:50A	Hodel and Ellen - unintelligible conversation.
33½-34½	12:00P	Hodel and Ellen - unintelligible conversation.
	12:00P	Sullivan Relieves Morgan
	12:35P	Hodel to Ellen "You got crumbs all over my bed. Will you get them off without getting them on the floor.
34½-36	12:42P	Hodel dials phone (recorded) WY 2064 (?) hangs up and dials again. No response.
36-38	12:50P	Phone rings, Hodel answers (recorded) "How are the kid and fishing". Apparently talking to his wife, Dorothy. "I'll come down this evening, around 8 o'clock.

HODEL FILE - 89   89

38-41½   1:01P   Phone rings. Hodel answers (recorded) Water running a
                 conversation is unintelligible. Sounds like talking ab
                 sale of house. Will show by appointment only. Call
                 about 1:45 PM.

41½-44   1:21P   Phonerings. Hodel answers (recorded) "Your'e talking
                 over a tapped line. Oh yes, it's been tapped for a lon
                 time. I'll be home for the next hour. Be sure and com

44-45   1:26P   Hodel dials phone (recorded) Asking for theater seats.

45-46   1:27P   Hodel dials phone (recorded) "I want Gittleson's.
                 I want 2 front centers for Martha Graham." He got them
                 at $4.80 each.

46-46½   1:28P   Hodel dials phone (recorded) Asking about seats for
                 Martha Graham.

46½-47   1:38P   Hodel dias phone (recorded) Asks for medical desk.

         1:44P   Ellen advises Hodel party there to see house. Hodel
                 tells Ellen to take her back and show her the rooms on
                 other side, that he will be out in a few minutes
                 (from bathroom)

         1:58P   Hodel talking to lady about sale of house.

47-48   2:10P   Talking to Ellen (recorded) Not intelligible.

         2:25P   Quiet.

         2:35P   Man talking in some other part of house. sounds like t
                 salesman who talked all thru yesterday p.m.

         2:41P   Man still talking.

48-60   2:45P   Man still talking (recorded) talking to Hodel about so
                 woman. Mentions Barbara Sherman. Dorothy Black (?)
                 Som thing about Santa Barbara. Hodel - "She called me
                 this morning. She's coming over this P.M." Man-"You
                 had pretty good success with some of those dames I fixe

90

2:55P	Spool #31 runs out.
2:55P	Man continues talking about his blood pressure and going into army.
3:05P	Phone rings. Hodel answers - "It's on Franklin near Normandie". Talked about renting apt. or apt. and a single studio room available. 75.00 for room. Wire breaks while ~~recordin rewin~~ rewinding spool 31 at time 32.
3:10P	Phone rings - Hodel answers "giving directions as to how to get to his home".
3:25P	Phone rings-Hodel answers "Thank you for calling".
3:26P	Hodel to man "In about 2 or 3 weeks I'll probably be on way abroad.
3:27P	Man and Hodel still talking about man getting into serv: Hodel tells him if he can get even as a private xhe show He asks Hodel if he got back in and continued to handle tea around bay area if it would make his blood pressure worse. Talks a lot about "Corky" apparently wife or friend of salesman. Hodel tells man he would pay him 1000.00 if he'd sell Hodel's house. They leave to walk around the house.
3:40P	Man and Hodel again talking about blood pressure.
3:44P	Phone rings 2 times, answered in some other part of the house.
3:50P	Phone rings 2 times - answered otherpart of house.
4:00P	Quiet for past 15 minutes.
4:06P	Jim McGrath, D.A.'s office on duty.
4:00P	Salesman and Hodel talking again. Something about a $15.00 check the salesman wanted Hodel to give him - ma

HODEL FILE - 91

4:00P out to a Joe. Which the salesman wants to show his
landlady. The check - also salesman told Hodel he was
broke - told Hodel how this AM he went into a restauran
he always eats at and had breakfast for 55¢ - then walk
over to the magazine section - looked at some magazines
and left without paying - both got a big laugh out of t

Spool 32

4:14P A Mr Rappart phones Hodel regarding house.

5:27P Salesman leaves

4:44P Spool 32 on

4:57P Someone calls (a girl) re. a room for 2 - Hodel explain
house.

5:05P Hodel shows house to some woman - said"I've rented one
the rooms since talking to you."

5:35P Phone rings 2 times, answered in another part of house.
Not able to hear conversation.

5:55P Hodel in conversation with the man with the German accel
trying to record, however reception is very poor.
(tried 2 min. of recording, but shut it off - can't
understand)

5:58P Conversation ends - not heard anymore.

6:02P Hodel receives a phone call regarding the house - could
not make out (racket and noise is loudest ever
heard) Sounds like he rented the other room - said "let
me have your phone, yes 27829 - No, since there are 4 of
you, it would add too much of a load on the phones."
It appears 4 girls are moving in - one by the name of
Miss Maxwell it sounded like.

HODEL FILE - 92

6:40P   Phone rang - Hodel to some woman (recorded) no info.
         obtained.

6:55P   Some man in conversation with someone on phone - not
         Hodel (recorded) the salesman who had dinner with Hodel
         got some phone number 89581. Prefix not mentioned - th
         is the phone number of another girl - Hodel came back
         phone rang - someone calling re. the house - the addres
         of the girl is Santa Monica Blvd and Cahuenga. Motion
         Picture Industry PBX operator.

7:22P   Phone rings once - no conversation - must have been
         answered on extension.

7:25P   Hodel in conversation with one of the girs who was goin
         to move in-her phone number is HU 27289 - some indicati
         they may not take the room. Hodel is to phone in the A
         could not ascertain her name.

7:35P   Hodel phones party named Mickey - said he would like he
         to read him some poetry tonight - asked how her energy
         was. Started talking very low - could not make out.
         "I'm a easy listener". (Presume he's talking to a s
         can't hear clear - said would she like to be observed -
         frustration and complexes-mentioned something about
         relationship with me - I'm sure of myself - told her 2
         stories.

8:00P   Meyer, LAPD, on duty

8:30P   Talking in some other room.

8:40P   Hodel talking to two women who he is trying to sell or
         rent house - said he would rent for $90.00 month. Two
         unmarried sisters-sounds as though one can't speak Engl
         Said he had the studio rented to some woman painter.

HODEL FILE - 93

8:40P   One other room to some other woman, asks them to come back and look tomorrow. He won't be home, but house-keeper will.xxxxx Change spool.

Spool 33
9:03P   Other man came in - women still there. Hodel introduce man as his business manager - women leave. Hodel goesx other part of house.

9:12P   Hodel and man talking - man has accent. Hodel takes him to bedroom and talks in low voices - said something some case being cold - seemed to talk about tax on sale of clinic - can't hear too well. (Recorded-hope can hear better) Hodel gave man Two phone numbers, his OL 3476 some office TR x52x 1252. PBX operator comes back and other man who has been around for awhile. All three tal' about some business deal - can't figure it out - say something about China.

9:40P   Phone rang - Hodel answered. Didn't say xxxx anything. Talking about selling something.

9:50P   Sounds as though 2 men left. Hear one person around.

10:00P   All 3 back. Hodel says he knows 4 girls in Burbank Two are 19 and two are 20, who are practising oriental dances and are going to Mexican and Latin America. Hodel asks man with accent if he thinks they would go o' down there. Hodel talks as though he has a contract an will go along.

10:37P   2 men talking - one telling about place he lives, but i leaving other can have it. Didn't mention any address.

10:45P   Two people talking in one room, and a lot of racket in another room. (recorded) but couldn't understand.

HODEL FILE - 94

	10:45P	2 men leave. Hodel says he won't be home tomorrow.
	11:15P	Quiet, Hodel and ellen around.
	11:45P	Hodel typing.
3-5-50	12:12A	Phone rings. Hodel answers, "Yes honey. I am painting some furniture. I am a great lover of honesty."
		Talks about car other party bought. Said he would like to get one but couldn't pay cash. Asks about taking th car someplace. Break car in andyou in at same time.
		Talks about a poker game.
	12:45A	Quiet. Hodel still moving around.
	1:15A	Quiet. Hodel still moving around.
	1:30A	All quiet. Think Hodel went to bed in another part of house.
	1:45A	LAPD Wean,relieves Meyer.
	2:00A	Apparently still in bed. No movement of any kind.

Spool 34
0-

	8:00A	Hronek, D.A.'s office on duty
	8:30A	All quiet.
	9:00A	All quiet.
	9:30A	Phone rang 2 times, didn't hear anyone answer.
	10:00A	All quiet.
	10:30A	All quiet.
	10:40A	Hear child's voice in background - very faint
	11:19A	Phone rang 3 times, child's voice in background - must answered in another room.
	11:59A	Hear Hodel humming and moving around the desk.
	12:00P	Releived by Jack Egger, D.A.'s office.
	12:05P	Bathroom noises - woman humming in background.

HODEL FILE - 95

	12:06p	Woman greeted someone at front door, coult not pick up conversation.
	12:15P	Conversation in background, cannot pick it up conversation between Hodel and other man.
	12:20P	Turned on radio, playing symphony music.
	12:22P	Typewriting can be heard over the symphony - man coughin
	1 PM	Radio still on (symphony) typewriting still going on.
	1:2 5 P	Phone rang, cannot hear conversation because of radio.
1½	1:35P	Phone rang - recorded - conversation with some one whom he told to "come over after work tomorrow".
	1:40P	Typewriting resumed by Hodel.
	1:50P	Knock on door, Hodel let woman in-Conversation ensued
3½		(tried to record but it was background)
	2:00P	Hodel seems to be opening and closing drawers. Typewri resumed.
6½-7	2:10P	Hodel in conversation with man and woman, but cannot pi it up very well. Too far in background - seem to be talking about photography of a surrelistic nature. Hod shows some xxx pictures of his to the two people - also talking about renting some suites of rooms in his place Man has a definite spanish accent, asked Hodel about Spanish doctors in this area. Hodel mentioned leaving in a "couple of months" Attempt to record this convers tion proved futile because it was too much in background Hode again started talking about photographs with the people - part of conversation is recorded.
11½	3:00PM	Pictures seemed to be of Japanese girls.
	3:03P	The two people left.

HODEL FILE - 96

3:05P   Another man came in - talked to Hodel fəx about
a red headed girl who may live there with her mother.
Both seemed interested in if the girl was over 18 or no⃝
Man asked Hodel if when he went to Santa Monica if he w⃝
going to stay there or not.

15   3:20P   Hodel called up a girl named Carol, asked her about buyi⃝
a couch from her.

16   Hodel bought the couch from her for $35.00 and said it
a deal, now you only ow me $50. and said goodby and hun⃝
up.

3:25P   Phone rang - must have been answered in other room.

3:25P   Hodel left the room - radio still on in background.

3:33P   Hodel back in room, some typing and moving about.
No conversation.

4:00P   Relieved by Jim McGrath, D.A.'s office

Spool 35

J. Egger had trouble with other spool No. 34, it had br⃝
took same off and replaced with #35, lost some of the s⃝
in removing.

5:30P   Hodel and salesman in conversation. "Can't make it"
Salesman said, it's down in the basement locked up. Th⃝
salesman talked about his blood pressure.

6:35P   Hodel and Ellen in conversation - not understood - mumk⃝

7:30P   Hodel and Ellen in conversation - mumbling faint - can'⃝
hear.

7:50P   Phone call to Hodel from Pat, said, "Wait a minute, I'⃝
be with you. Hudson 27829, is her phone. Hodel to cal⃝
her in A.M.

8:00P   Meyer on duty, LAPD

HODEL FILE - 97

97

	8:40P	Hodel called Joe, asked him if he didn't want the room. Hodel had a chance to rent it to two "sweet"young girls one goes to U.S.C., and the other is a Secretary for Prudential Life Insurance Company.
	8:45P	Calls some woman and talks about renting part of house to her - says he is going abroad soon - makes appointment for 12:45 tomorrow to show house.
	9:15P	All quiet.
	9:45P	All quiet.
	10:15P	All quiet.
	10:45P	All quiet.
	11:15P	All quiet.
	11:45P	All quiet.
3-6-50	12:15A	All quiet.
	12;45A	All quiet.
	1:15A	All quiet.
	1:45A	All quiet.
	2:00A	Brechel, LAPD, on duty, all is quiet.
	2:20A	Several odd sounds in background, sounds like trumpet o an elephant.
	2:45A	Noises in background indicate someone working around, probably in studio.
	3:10A	Hodel enters from rear, part of house, goes to lavatory urinates.
	3:15A	Hodel goes to bed.

HODE FILE -   97-A

Spool 35

3-6-50

5:10A	Hodel gets out of bed. Goes to other part of house for a minute, then returns to bed.
8:00A	J. McGrath, D.A.'s office on duty.
9:40A	Hodel up - talking to Ellen - said come on let's get up. going. ~~Gave~~ Gave her hell for being in room for 10 minutes times.
9:55A	Phone rings - Hodel answers-about renting room.
10:15A	Ordering blankets from Broadway Hollywood.
10:35A	Hodel asking for phone number of owner's Realty's Servic
10:50A	Hodel ~~inxSx~~ and Spanish man talking about "refiguring a job" of some kind in the house.
11:30A	Hodel phones Menlo 46516 - did not hear any conversatior
12:03A	Joe phoned - Hodel talked about callers in the house.
12:00noon	Snyder - D.A.'s office on duty
12:40P	Hodel calls regarding houses for sale - hangs up and raises hell with Ellen over nothing.
12:55P	Shirley Throckmorten - student - calls - talks to Hodel regarding being student in Hodel's class (whatever that is) both move to part of house where talk is un-intelligible - both return and Hodel suggests they sit in his car and talk - to which party agrees.

HODEL FILE - 98   99

3-6-50   Snyder, D.A.'s office on duty

No wire
No recording

1:40P   Both return to room - talk on medical problems.

1:45P   Hodel answers phone regarding Miss Davis - ṃṃ on positic
           with some Dr. 1/31/50 date mentioned by Hodel.

1:50P   Resumes conversation with prospect - possibly partners i
           business - talk re. 2 party phone as to costs, etc. -
           apparently selling "lady" bill of goods.

2:30P   Phone rings - Hodel answers - not important.

2:30P   Resume talk with lady suspect "?" or prospect.

3:10P   Gal still there - conversation unintelligible.
           (Belle and Bimson playing back recordings)

3:25P   Hodel phones - wants specimen picked up at 3684 7th Ave.

3:30P   Gal leaves - will return.

3:55P   Hodel does some typing - also talks to Ellen - gives her
           some more hell for free.

4:15P   Hodel still typing - (monotonous, isn't it?)

4:25P   Phone rings - Hodel answers.

4:30P   Snyder, off duty, Eggers on, D.A.'s office

4:45P   Hodel typing

5:00P   Hodel still typing

5:05P   Hodel goes out of room - all quiet.

5:15P   Hodel back, has another man with him - background
           conversation cannot pick-up.

5:25P   Woman enters - still in background.

5:30P   Everyone leaves room - all quiet.

5:35P   Hodel returns to the room-opens some drawers and leaves
           again - all quiet.

HODEL FILE - 99

5:40P	All quiet.
5:50P	Hodel back, with woman - woman talking about Painting he kitchen.
	Hodel talked about a woman named "Tracey Racapore" who attends UCLA who is renting rooms from him. Stated that "she is about 22 years of age, very nice girl who studie most of the time".
6:00P	Conversation continues - woman talking about renting roo
6:02P	Another man enters, conversation very much in the background.
6:05P	Hodel and girl talking - girl said she "would be afraid to live alone". Hodel said he would "protect her to the best of his ability". Girl said that she "would get ove being afraid, O.K."
6:15P	Hodel shows the girl some pictures of his; they seem to portraits of an abstract nature, conversation turns to photos.
6:15P	Man with accent, apparently spanish, comes into conversation.
6:20P	Everyone except Hodel leaves.
6:22P	Another woman comes in. Hodel tells her "to sit down ar take it easy for a minute".
6:30P	Hodel in background, conversation with woman.
6:35P	Woman leaves - Hodel alone working at desk. can hear occasional dog barking in background.
6:45P	Another woman enters, she and Hodel talk about renting
6:55P	rooms. Woman said she will call Hodel between 11 and 1? tomorrow, and leaves.

HODEL FILE - 100   ¹⁰¹

7:05P	Hodel alone - working at desk - typing
7:30P	Hodel still alone - moving about room. Hodel called Menlo 46517 from operator - no answer. Hodel called another number - could not get it, told the girl his
7:45P	new phone number would be <u>OL 3476</u>, and that he was "keeping it secret. He asked the girl if she and "Milli would come over soon.
7:47P	A woman comes into Hodel's room; he asked her "when her mother was coming over". The girl said, this eveni? She said her mother is Mrs Alica De Varora, and her name is Villa De Varora. Hodel stated that his type of work is Administrative Medicine, and at present he has a laboratory and has done a lot of work for the government overseas, etc.
8:00P	Egger, D.A.'s office off duty.
8:00P	Wean, LAPD, on duty.
8:10P	Hodel moving around, no conversation.
8:20P	Woman talking to Hodel. Can't understand.
8:25P	Woman leaves - man enters - talks with Hodel about moral of spanish girls. Hodel tells man he should have seen his Chinese collection which was worth $100,000.
8:30P	Man calls woman on phone and tells her he is going out with Hodel - to have some drinks.
8:35P	Hodel suggests they go to a Chinese place. They leave.
9:20P	Someone enters - then could hear woman crying. Phonograph turned on. No conversation.
10:45P	Phonograph. Still playing and someone typewriting.
10:50P	Phone rings - unable to hear with music.
11:05P	Hodel tells Ellen to pack everything in a box and

HODEL FILE - 82 ~~102~~

	11:50AM	Hodel working around desk
	11:55AM	Hodel said to Ellen "Take the suitcase down and have it fixed".
	11:55P	Hodel started typing
	12:00noon	Hodel still typing
	12:00noon	Sullivan, D.A.'s office relieves Eggers
	12:15P	Hodel talking to Ellen - unintelligible
0-1	12:30P	Hodel dials - asks for number of Santa Fe - then dials (recorded) much racket
1-4½	12:32P	Hodel dials S.P. Rwy. - (recorded) wants info on trains, sounds like to Arizona, to Gila Bend, Ariz. Leave 8:30 at night - asks for fare - $12.04
	12:45P	Typing
	12:55P	Hodel dials phone - asks about OPA regulations in LA "Does rent control still cover L.A. House was built in 192 Place has never been registered. Well, it's a big house, a I thought I'd divide it up into rooms and apartments. The name is Harvey; Owner George Harvey, 5121 Franklin.
	12:57P	Hodel dials phone - asks for American Red Cross - Call me a OL 3476
	1:05P	Hodel typing
	1:12P	Hodel talking to Ellen - "I can take that package down and mail. Also Tomar's. Is Tomar's ready. I got to take a trip in the car and can mail the package.
	1:15P	Hodel talking in a low voice to some girl. Said something about taking something to her mother. Conversation continued for about 5 minutes, but unable to get any of it due to low tones.
	1:26P	Conversation resumes, but still unintelligible.

HODEL FILE - ~~83~~ / 07

	1:55P	Typing
	2:00P	Radio on. Hodel and woman talking. Cannot understand due to radio and racket. Sounds like someone interested in house.
	2:12P	Emergency vehicle passing. Conversation with woman continues. Still unintelligible.
	2:21P	Hodel talking to a woman - radio in background and conversation unintelligible
4½-6	2:22P	Started recording. Believe woman to be Ellen
	2:25P	Conversation with Ellen continues.
	2:28P	Phone rings - Ellen answers "Whose calling - just a moment" can't hear anything further.
	2:30P	Hodel talking "I would like a check on OL 3476 - when can you get a service man out".
	2:40P	Typing - and radio still playing
	2:50P	Phone - Hodel answers - He gives his name and address
	3:15P	Quiet
	3:25P	Hodel talking, unable to understand
	3:45P	Hodel to Ellen - something about reservations. Sounds like Ellen to go to Arizona
	4:00P	Hronek, D.A.'s office on duty
	4:30P	All quiet
	5:00P	All quiet, only water running in the bathroom
	5:10P	Conversation in the background, impossible to understand
7-12	5:30P	Hodel talking with some woman (recorded) too much disturbance to understand.
	6:00P	Hear Hodel moving around - talk in the background
	6:30P	All quiet

HODEL FILE - 84 *103*   104

	6:57P	Hodel starts typing
	7:00P	All quiet
12-13	7:08P	Hodel dials - gets wrong number - tries again (recorded)
		Hodel leaves the room
	7:30P	All quiet
13-14	7:31P	Phone rings 5 times - answered by Ellen in another part of the house - couldn't hear at all
	8:00P	Hronek off duty - all quiet
	8:00P	Wean, LAPD, on duty
	8:10P	Talking in background - can't understand.
	9:05P	Talking in background - can't understand.
	10:00P	Hodel messing around in toilet - no conversation
14-30	10:30P-11:25P	Man enters - they talk, can't make out too well (recorded)
30-34	11:40P	Hodel talking about some plans, but can't make out (recorded

3-8-50

	2:00A	Brechel, LAPD, on duty - All quiet. Hodel probably in bed can hear snoring.
	3:00A	All is quiet
	4:00A	All is quiet
	5:00A	Male voice in background, too far away to understand. Sound lasted about a minute then all quiet again. Hodel still snoring.
	6:30A	Ellen moving around.
	8:00A	J. McGrath, D.A.'s office on duty
	8:30A	Phone rings - Hodel answers - about the "Packard jalopy" starting hard talking to some mechanic about fixing up the car. Said "I will see you later - about 10:30A or 11 AM regarding the car - having it fixed".

HODEL FILE - 85 104

¹⁰⁵

	10:30A	Conversation over phone with his wife Dorothy - she was complaing about money-he said he is broke - can't pay mortgage on the house this month - has no money coming in' from sounds of conversation bad feelings may be developing. Also spoke of going to see a Mrs. La Cour. Hodel was to write her.
	12:25P	Called Lou regarding the Packard - said would be down in five minutes.
	12:36P	Called Postal information for information regarding pka postal service with the capital of Tibet.
	12:36P	Snyder, D.A.'s office on duty
		All quiet - Hodel is having car repaired - apparently no on in houe at all.
	2:30P	Phone rings 9 times - no one answers.
	4:00P	Hronek, D.A.'s office on duty
34-39	4:19P	Telephone conversation with someone (recorded)
39-40		Phone Company to disconnect the extension OL 3476 - should have been disconnected today, tomorrow expects to work only 12-2 PM - or Friday, he'll stay home himself.
	5:10P	Hodel starts typing
40-42	5:30P	Hodel carries a conversation with another man - phone rang and unkn man left.
	6:15P	Hodel dials, asks to have someone call him.
42-44	7:15P	Hodel dials - asks for Dr Friedner, dials another 3787 So. Vermont - Friedner's address
	7:30P	Hodel typing like mad.
	8:00P	Hronek off duty.
	8:00P	Meyer, LAPD, on duty

HODEL FILE - ~~86~~ /0√   106

	8:10P	Hodel phones someone and asks name and exact title of Chief of States of Burma and Tibet - wants to know how they are addressed. Name of Minister Public Health of Burma - goes back to typing.
	8:45P	Phone rang 3 times, didn't hear anyone answer - has been quiet for past 20 minutes.
	8:54P	Phone rang 3 times, didn't hear anyone answer.
	9:30P	All quiet
	10:00P	All quiet
	10:15P	Hodel typing
	10:45P	Hodel still typing
	11:15P	Hodel still moving around
	11:45P	All quiet
3-9-50	12:15A	All quiet. Hodel snoring
	12:45A	All quiet. Hodel still snoring
	1:15A	All quiet. Hodel still snoring
	1:45A	All quiet. Hodel still snoring
	2:00A	Brechel, LAPD, on duty. All is quiet except for Hodel snoring.
	6:10A	Woman - may be Ellen Moving around house
	8:00A	J. McGrath, D.A.'s office on duty
	9:15A	Someone knocking on a door 3 times
	9:35A	Phone call - couldnot make much out. Hodel asked"if you were going to pick that up".
	9:50A	Hodel phoned Telephone Company to have extension of OL 3476 disconnected.

HODEL FILE - 87/06

107

10:00AM   Hodel has a male patient - gave him Methrolate to put 3
           drops in each eye, one time a day. Hodel is talking with
           man with German accent - talking about going to the auction
           and buying and selling things - talking about buying paints

10:03AM   Phone call - Hodel answered - nothing said - just "yes,yes"

10:07AM   Another phone call. Hodel talks to someone about selling
           lumber - pressure cooker, and odd and ends.

10:40AM   Hodel makes phone call - for Repair Department - complained
           about a condensor - sputtering.

10:55AM   Officer Bimson and Sgt. Belle checked Hodel's residence for
           license plates to find out who man with German accent is -
           the following plates were in sun in front of Hodel's house
           75 P 519 - 35 Packard F.E. Mattoon - 251 S. Lucerne, L.A;
           9 P 3938 - 47 Chev. Willie Wheeler, 4461 Towne Ave., L.A.
           8R5 420 - 41 Ford Conv. Violet Jean Wallen - 2055 N.
           New Hampshire, L.A.
           60A8 150 - 36 Packard, Marie L. Valla - 2212 N. Nella Vista,
           L.A.

11:30AM   All quiet around house.

12:03AM   Hodel calls a Mr. Kurst or Hurst - talking about photo-
           stats - said Mr. Good has pictures - also the photographers
           name is Ackerman.

12:15AM   Phone rings - Hodel says "I love you very much. I'm at
           the house"or something like that. "I'll see you at 1:15.

12:16PM   Hodel phones - a Margaret said "he has a 2 PM appointment."

12:20AM   Sullivan, D.A.'s office on duty.

1:15AM   Phone rings. No one answers. Quiet since 12:25.

1:30AM   Phone rings - no one answers.

2:05AM   Someone walking around.

HODEL FILE - 88 107   108

2:20 AM	Hodel talking with some man. Conversation unintelligible (much static and noise in machine).
2:25 AM	Water running.
2:39 AM	Hodel dials phone "asks for Mr. Kurst(?) "Kurst not in? I'll call back".
2:50 AM	Hodel talking to someone by phone about an inlay china box. Apparently trying to sell some China piece he has.
2:51 AM	Hodel phones. "Hello, brother, good. I'll have some of those special manhattans for you. Take my new number, OL 3476. Give me a ring and drop by around the cocktail hour. I gave it to Mr. Kirsh (?)
3:00 AM	Phone rings - Hodel answers "Sure, I'll be here." Conversation in very low tones.
3:17 PM	Hodel asks for number at 5101 Hollywood Blvd. Then dials number. "Are my trousers and shirts ready? I'll stop by for them".
3:50 PM	Hodel phones someone - states he is calling for a Mrs. Chajud who wants to share a luxurious apartment with some girl. He gives this party his phone number, and address.
3:51 AM	Hodel calls. Gives a rental listing to share an apartment. "Calling for Mrs. De Chajud(?) Mrs. C. has a 19 yr. old daughter, and she wants some one-preferably a young college student-to share apartment. Someone who wants an artistic setup. Mrs. C. is just here from Costa Rica, but speaks good English. Mrs. De Chajud - $35.00, 5121 Franklin by appointment.

HODEL FILE - ~~89~~ /08

109

44-51	3:55 AM	Hodel dials (recorded) - (very interesting) repitition of above about Mrs. Chajud and daughter sharing a luxurious apartment in a $100,000. house.
		<u>4:00-8:00A - Hronek on duty, D.A.'s office</u>
	4:02 PM	A woman comes in. Hodel - "How are you". Much static. Unable to understand. Hear Hodel again on phone talking about apartment.
	4:20 PM	Hodel dials phone - again talks to a rental agency. Repeats his Mrs De Chajud pitch about sharing an apartment. Wants a 19 or 20 yr. old girl. Some hammering and sawing in background.
	4:25 PM	Hodel dials phone - another rental agency.
	4:30 PM	Call to another agency
	4:35 PM	Another one
	4:38 PM	Hodel dials - gets another agency
	4:41 PM	Hodel dials - gets another agency
	4:42 PM	Hodel calls another agency about a girl to share the apartme
	4:50 PM	Phone rings - Hodel answers - something about a box he could use over the weekend
	4:57 PM	Phone rang - Hodel answered. "The sooner we have that audition the better. Sunday will be a good time. Do you know of any place where I could make arrangements?"
	5:05 PM	Talking to some woman (new housekkeeper) about showing her the secret of the lock, and about going out for awhile.
	6:00 PM	All quiet.
	7:00 PM	All quiet.
	7:30 PM	Phone rang 3 times - no answer
	7:55 PM	Hodel moving around the house and bathroom.

HODEL FILE - ~~89~~ /08

HODEL FILE - ~~90~~/09   110

51	8:00PM	Meyer, LAPD on duty

8:02PM Hodel turns radio on - low talking - unable to hear - is on phone talking to someone about a sore throat. Said something about Mexico - if she was OK - could probably leave tomorrow night

8:20PM Hodel calls Orchid 22032 - asks for Marian - then talks to someone about Marian - going to Frisco.

8:23PM Hodel calls Sunset 16510 - asks for Harry.

8:24PM Hodel calls Sunset 33419 - talks to Harry - asks if he knows where he can get in touch with Jonathin Usher? Says he is a ham radio operator, and Hodel wants to receive a message from Tibet in about 2 to 4 weeks.

8:55PM Hodel talks to Harry again - same subject

9:45PM Hodel still typing and moving around

10:45PM Hodel still moving around

3-10-50 12:15A One or two men and about same amount of women - Talking to Hodel. Hard to understand - something about a place in Mexico not too far from Arizona - good roads - something about a Whore House, or sanatarium. One man seems to be a doctor. Talking about she at Camarillo. Hodel - "She was going to shoot me and commit suicide "Tamara" (way it sounded) Talking about fishing trip to Mexico 228 miles from Phoenix, Arizona - seem to be looking at map-mentioned Sonora, Mexico - other party leaves 1:15A - says he will leave Hodel know about noon tomorrow - Friday - about trip.

HODEL FILE - 9̶1̶ //0

2:00A	Wean, LAPD, on duty
2:15A	Hodel apparently gone to bed. All quiet.
6:15A	Hodel getting up - moving around house.
8:00AM	J. McGrath, D.A.'s office on duty. All quiet.
8:45AM	Phone rang 2 times - could not hear an answer
9:00AM	Phone rang - Hodel said, "Hello - yes - how's things" hung up. Hodel is up and around.
9:10AM	Hodel and some woman in short conversation - could not understand - then they went to rear of the house.
9:15AM	Hodel makes phone call - asks for extension 372 - Mr. Rolley or Ragey - about his export business - about an orde: Hodel had placed - nothing else mentioned as to products, e'
10:10AM	Phone call from Ted. Hodel asked "do you know a Dr. Donald, L.A. Terey, or L.A. Perez at a mission - address may be 56 Martan or Martana Rd. Not in private practice - asked how many siamanese practitioners there were. Told Ted first chance he has to phone him to have dinner - as he wants to talk tohim
10:20AM	Phone call to Mabel - asked if Irwin was working - asked he: to have him come by - also said would like to see you some- time - asked ›er about pains in her stomach.
10:25AM	Phoned Telephone Company to pick up some old telephone directories.
10:27AM	Phone call - something about a short stocky man picking up a deposit.
10:32AM	Hodel phones someone to pick up something - could not make out what.

	10:33AM	Phone call received by Hodel - said maybe going away for the weekend - said to phone him at 4 PM - he would know
	11:07AM	Phone call received - Hodel answered - sounds like planning a trip - asked when can you get away - will phone you prefixes not obtained-numbers are 84435 and 81831
	11:27AM	Hodel phones Orchard 22033 - no answer
	11:30AM	Phone call received - something about dropping off some clothes - said again he may leave town - also asked for a book containing names and addresses
	11:35AM	Hodel makes phone call-too much static and Hodel too far away to make out.
~~3-11-50~~	12:25P	Sgt Belle - said he has found out the man with the German accent is one Baron Herringer - a supposed ex-German - Baron. The two new girls are Vilma (age 19) and Sonia (age 15) Said had moved in with their mother. 2 sisters.
	1:15PM	Burns, D.A.'s office on duty
	2:00PM	Hodel returned to house.
	2:20PM	Hodel talking to man about income tax with-holding, etc.
	2:35PM	Hodel talks on phone (received call)-too much static.
	2:45PM	Hodel received phone call "She's coming over. Does she know the name. I'll have her call you as soon as she gets here.
	2:48PM	Resumed talk of Income tax, withholding-with man (unnamed)
	4:10PM	Hodel called OR 27023, No answer.
	4:15PM	Income taxconsultant left.
	4:20PM	Hodel received call from patient about stmach.
	4:25PM	Woman entered house - no conversation with herl
	4:45PM	Hronek, D.A.'s office on duty.

HODEL FILE - 93-112   113

51½	4:55PM	Phone rang 2 times - answered in a whisper
	5:05PM	Conversation with a woman - distant - hard to understand - toilet being flushed 3 times in a row
41½-52		Spool ran out just when Hodel talked with Joe. Joe still talks -"that's one of the conditions of my probation." A woman present.

SPOOL #36

0-14	4:20PM	Mixed conversation - Hodel answered the phone. Hodel called Superior 84425 - Superior 81831 - conversation about a plane trip over the weekend.
14-17	5:59PM	Seems to have a woman patient. Woman - ST 45442 - seems
17-53		like Hodel and party are leaving for Mexico tonight.
	6:40PM	Hodel called Charles about cancelling the trip to Mexico because he can't line up 4 reliable people. Going out for supper - woman called another party - who was willing to loan his car for the trip. Finally decided that they'll leave Wednesday night. Hodel showing the map and pictures the woman.
	6:50P	The phone rang - Hodel answered "Hello Betty"- Toilet being flushed - can't understand
	7:05P	Hodel dials information "What's the number of 5101 Hollywoo Blvd.
	7:20P	Phone rang 7 times - no answer.
	7:32P	Phone rang 4 times - no answer
	7:57P	Phone rang 5 times - no answer
	8:00P	Meyer, L.A.P.D. on duty. All quiet.
	8:32P	Phone rang 3 times - didn't hear anyone answer - sounds as though someone talking in another room.

HODEL FILE - 94 113   114

	10:05P	Phone rang 3 times - no one answered.
3-11-50	1:00A	Hodel comes home - sounds like a woman with him - can't understand them - in another room. Sounds like it may be his ex-wife. Can't understand what talking about.
	1:35A	Sounds as though Hodel is at his desk.
	1:45A	Hodel starts typing.
	2:00A	Wean, LAPD, on duty
	2:15A	Hodel moving around - no conversation
	2:45A	Hodel apparently gone to bed - can hear snoring.
	7:40A	All quiet.
	8:00A	J. McGrath, D.A.'s office on duty.
	8:10A	Phone call to Hodel - who said "OK will see you at 9 AM".
	9:30A	Phone call - Hodel said "See me Monday or Tuesday. I'm going fishing over the weekend.
	10:07A	Woman phoning Santa Monica 42421 - asked how the children were, said "I went to the doctor's yesterday and I did not feel good so I stayed with George last night. He is driving down later, and I'll be down then. (Sounded like Dorothy-Hodel's ex-wife)
	10:40A	Hodel and German in conversation. Can't understand as woman in bathroom - running water and making all kinds of noises.
	10:50A	Hodel and German talking - Hodel wants to rent a 26 room lo near Mexecali in Mexico. Where President Comache of Mexico built to have conference with Roosevelt. He wants to make a rest home 300 air miles from L.A. 500 by car.

HODEL FILE - ~~95-114~~

10:55A	Phone rings 2 times - answered in rear of house - could not hear the German talking to Hodel about a man with nervous troubles (the German talks as though he is a doctor i.e., in medical terms)
11:45A	Sullivan, D.A.'s office on duty. Hodel and woman talking in background. ~~Believe his ex-wife, Dorothy.~~
12:10P	Mrs. Hodel doing a lot of talking, but apparently in some other part of house. Sounds as though she might be reading from a book or script. She's been talking for the past 10 minutes.
12:15P	Woman stops her reading or talking.
12:35P	Phone rings 3 times - possibly answered in some other part of house.
1:30P	Hear woman talking in background. Sounds like a woman and child.
1:40P	Man talking in background. Sounds like the talkative tea salesman.
1:43P	Typing.
1:55P	Typing by someone - not Hodel - Not as adept as Hodel. No conversation
1:59P	Woman dials phone. Sounded like she said, "This is Elsie". Talked about Vincent Price. Also, about M.G.M. Talked about John getting her a job. "Say Bob", I found a story. A story of a black saint, a negro. Do you know John Farrow? I thought of him because of his Catholicism. I met him years ago. I have the babies down at the beach. But, I'd love to see you. (t must be Dorothy talking) You're at home all day. Oh, wonderful darling" then "I'll get to see you"
2:05P	End of conversation.

HODEL FILE - 96~~115~~   116

	2:15P	Hodel talking. Unintelligible
	2:25P	Typing
	3:15P	Hodel and Dorothy conversing in background. Getting ready to leave.
	3:55P	Quiet reigns supreme.
	3:55P	Littleton, D.A.'s office relieves Sullivan

SPOOL 37

	4:00P	Hodel typing
	4:11P	Hodel calls "Come In" Undistinguishable conversation with woman. Typing stops.
	4:13P	Woman out, Hodel walking around.
	4:20P	Undistinguishable words from woman. Heavy banging sound like wood being wrenched loose, then typing resumed. More wrenching sounds after typing stops.
0-10	4:24P	Woman patient apparently. Short professional conversation. Phone call regarding flight by plane. Asks if party would "like to go down there tonight". Puts a woman on phone for conversation with caller. Hodel says he can "go tonight" on a flight. Woman tells caller that prospect of trip is "wonderful". Apparently a flight to Mexico. Undistinguishable chatter with woman after phone hung up.
10-21		
	4:35P	Phone rings. Woman answers. Undistinguishable conversation because of loud wrenching noises. Bathroom sounds – running water, flushing toilet. Hodel says "we drive (or ride) all night". Her answer undistinguishable.
	4:45P	Phone bell (?) rings twice. No one answers. Undistinct mummering between Hodel and woman. Woman calls, "Doctor!" General moving around in background. Undistinct conversation Hodel and woman over wrenching sounds. He tells her that

HODEL FILE - 97-116

117

sxx	something "is in her closet". More indistinct conversation with woman in background.
5:05P	Typing. Asks some woman (patient?) "let me have your address and phone number, please". Answer undistinguishable. He leaves, then apparently returns after indistinct chatter with a "Merl" (?) in background.
5:10P	Goes to background and calls "Ferrero!2(?) followed by indistinct chatter like some kind of instructions. Returns and typing is resumed.
5:15P	Calls "Come in, Rose (?) and get out there". Woman's voice indistinguishable, receding to background. Child's voice indistinct in background. Child's voice - indistinct.
5:25P	Typing. Leaves foreground, urinates, and flushes toilet. Undistinct talk in background - Hodel and woman. Hodel says "Next wekk - maybe make it Friday". Apparently woman patient. Hodel returns to foreground. Talk with woman undistinguishable.
5:35P	Typing, whistling as he does. Someone else moving around in background. Apparently he is not typing because he is talking indistinctly in background on phone. Says, "I'll be there and get it Tuesday night. I'll be looking for you". Rest of conversation not distinguishable because of typing. Says, "That's the only reason I'm going".
5:42P	Typing continuing in foreground. Outside traffic noises also interfering with conversation. Hodel and woman in background. Hodel says something about "Calexico". Woman says "Is there a road"? Hodel says, "The only road there is Typing stops.
5:53P	Indistinct conversation Hodel and woman.
6:00P	Moving about. No conversation.

HODEL FILE - 98-117   118

6:05P	All quiet, except outside traffic and possible very faint conversation in background.
6:08P	Conversation - man and woman in b.g. very faint and undistinguishable. Some faint movement around background.
6:14P	All quiet except outside traffic.
6:37P	Steady, rushing noise - possibly bath water or shower?
6:44P	Noise continues
6:50P	Noise continues. Vaccum cleaner?
7:05P	Noise may be defect in receiver, but if so, cannot determine same. Phoned Lt. Jemison, CR 14917, but no answer.
7:20P	Noise continues. Phoned Technician Braison at OL 9807. While talking with him, noise stopped.
7:22P	All quiet. Normal signal of outside traffic noises coming through. Dog barking.
8:00P	Littleton off duty.
8:00P	Meyer, LAPD, on duty
8:20P	Sounds like someone moving around.
10:20P	All quiet.

3-12-50	2:00AM	Brechel, LAPD, on duty. All is quiet.
	3:50AM	Someone moving around for a few minutes.
	8:00AM	Egger, D.A.'s office on duty.
	8:15AM	All quiet.
	8:20AM	Someone walking around, possibly upstairs, no voices.
	9:30AM	All quiet.
	10:00AM	All quiet.
	11:30AM	All quiet.
	12:00noon	Cimino, D.A.'s office on duty.
	12:05P	All quiet.
	1:00P	Radio is turned on. Someone is walking.

HODEL FILE - ~~99~~ 118

119

	1:10P	Voice in background is unintelligible.
		Radio is still on - music can hardly be heard.
	1:15P	Man and woman are talking, but reception is bad - can't understand.
	1:30P	Radio off - all is quiet.
	1:45P	Bathroom sounds - footsteps. Woman talks - unintelligible.
	3:00P	All quiet.
	4:20P	Cimino off.
	4:20P	Morgan, D.A.'s office, on duty
	5:45P	Telephone rang - no answer
	7:00P	Woman talking (unintelligible)
21½-23	7:30P	Man and woman conversing (about rooms in house)
	8:00P	Wean, LAPD, on duty
	8:15P	Telephone rings 2 times - stops - no conversation
	8:30P	Telephone rings - 2 times - stops - no conversation
	8:45P	Radio playing - someone moving around
	2:00A	Brechel, LAPD on duty. All is quiet.
	6:30A	Someone moving around house.
	8:00A	J. McGrath, D.A.'s office on duty
	9:40A	Phone rings 8 times - no answer
	11:45A	Phone rings 9 times - no answer
	12:05P	Phone rings 8 times - no answer
	12:05P	Snyder - D.A.'s office on duty
	12:50P	Phone rings - 7 times - no answer
	1:20P	Phone rings 6 times - no answer
	1:45P	Phone rings 6 times - no answer
	1:55P	Phone rings 8 times - no answer
	2:10P	Phone rings 6 times - no answer
	2:10P	Phone rings 6 times - no answer

HODEL FILE - ~~100~~ //9

	2:15P	Phone rings 5 times - no answer
	2:15P	Phone rings 12 times - no answer
	2:22P	Phone rings 9 times - no answer
	2:50P	Phone rings 6 times - no answer
	3:00P	Phone rings 10 times - no answer
	3:40P	Phone rings 4 times - no answer
	4:05P	Phone rings 6 times - no answer
	5:00P	Snyder off duty
		Wean, LAPD on duty. Someone moving around.
	5:15P	Phone rang 6 times - no answer, though some women are talki in the background and moving around
23	7:00P	All quiet
	8:00P	All quiet
3-14-50	2:00A	Brechel, LAPD, on duty, all quiet.
	5:00A	Someone enters. Sounds indicate it may be Hodel. Goes to desk, rustling of paper, probably going thru mail. Nope, I was wrong. He was on the can, reading and grunting, then flushes toilet.
	5:30A	Hodel walking around house.
	6:00A	All is quiet.
	6:20A	Female footsteps and voice in background
	6:50A	Hodel is snoring
	8:00A	J. McGrath, D.A.'s office on duty
	8:15A	Using a pretext - determined Hodel is back from Mexico.
	9:55A	Hodel receives a phone call - can't understand too much noise and mumbling.
	11:45A	Hodel up and moving around in the bathroom.
	12:00noon	Sullivan, D.A.'s office on duty
	12:05P	Water running. Apparently Hodel in bathroom.

HODEL FILE - 101/20

	12:25P	Phone rings - Hodel answers - about a rental.
	1:10P	Bell ringing - sounds like alarm clock turned off.
	1:15P	Man talking with Hodel - low tones - unable to understand. Conversation about 2 minutes and man leaves.
	1:45P	Door bell rings. Man talking to Hodel. They apparently go to some other part of house.
	1:46P	Phone rings 3 times - hear no answer. Possibly in some other part of house.
	1:55P	Hodel pays man. Gives him a check for $18.25 on a $16.50 bill. Man gives Hodel change and thanks him very much and is sorry he bothered him.
	2:50P	Man talking in background.
	3:00P	Someone hammering.
	3:05P	Phone rings 2 times. Hodel answers, but unable to hear any conversation.
	3:30P	Hodel typing.
	4:00P	Hronek on duty.
23-30	4:13P	Hodel answered over the phone about his fishing in Mexico and dropping Ellen off in some town. Hoping she won't have enough money to return - (recorded) Resumes typing.
30-33	6:17P	Joe cam in - (recorded)
	6:33P	Hodel makes a call to SUnset 16510 - no answer.
33	7:17P	Hodel calls SUnset 16510 again - no answer.
	8:00P	Meyer, LAPD, on duty. All quiet.
	8:30P	Phone rang 2 times, didn't hear anyone answer.
	9:00P	Hodel and some woman come in. Can't understand conversation.
	9:15P	Radio on. Hodel didn't turn it on, not his type of music - too loud.

HODEL FILE - 102 /2/

122

	9:36P	Hodel plays some records in Spanish - says were recorded during bombing of Barsalone, Spain - in spanish.
	9:53P	About 3 more females enter - sounded like Nickey or Mickey and her bunch, all talking or reading spanish.
	10:20P	Phone rang - Hodel answers "Hello Harry, I have been trying to get you". Females making too much noise - can't hear Hodel - said something about fishing in Mexico - radio on again.
	11:00P	Females and Hodel just talking.
	11:20P	Hodel telling about the place in Mexico - he talked about before - said he looked at it when he was down this last time - shows a picture of the place - showing on the map location of place.
	11:26P	Some man came in - seemed to know girls.
33-35½	11:30P	Hodel and man go in back room and talk. Couldn't hear too well - probably receiving order - will pick it up - sounded like will see each other 4 PM tomorrow. Man leaves - man's name "Chris".
	11:40P	Lot of talking and laughing.
	11:44P	Phone rang - Hodel answers - talks about place in Mexico. Said he had a mexican doctor friend down there, females making lot of noise - tells about fishing in Mexico. Say property will be for sale or lease in two months which about right time. Climate is perfect. Says money is in fishing, about 160 miles by road. Says will try to see him before he goes down to Mexico. Sounded like said "Bob"
3-15-50	12:05A	Hodel says he can get a plane - holds 4 people beside pilot can't hear too well.
	12:15A	Women left - Hodel moving around.
	2:00A	Brechl, LAPD, on duty. All quiet except for Hodel snoring.

HODEL FILE - #3/2

123

6:30A	Female moving around house.
8:00A	J. McGrath, D.A.'s office on duty.
9:30A	No noise, all quiet to present time.
9:50A	~~Noxnnixnxyxxiixxpxixt~~ Phone call - Hodel answers. Say's wait a minute - sounds like he is looking for some papers. Gave someone a phone number 32341 - could not get prefix.
10:02A	Charlotte, phones Hodel - said to phone him around 6 - just general conversation.
10:55A	Hodel and some man talking about colors. hard to understan Talking low. Also talking about plastic bottles, tops, also colors of the caps in bottles. Talking about putting liquid ~~liquor~~ in caps t test them. $16.00 a 1000 for plugs. 8 oz bottles - $27.50 a 1000. $20.00 a 1000 for caps. Non breakable bottles. Hodel going to Bullocks this afternoon - he tells salesman - Hodel talked to the buyer at Bullocks.
11:20A	Salesman leaves - all quiet.
11:45A	All quiet.
11:47A	Hodel called a Mr. Ramey - not in - left a call.
12:00noon	Hodel makes phone call - asks for Department #403 - said OK - thank you. Sullivan, D.A.'s office on duty.
12:45P	Phone rings 2xxtxx times - no answer heard. Possibly answered in some other part of home.
12:47P	Hodel talking on phone regarding Sero-logic Laboratories and bills against it. Hodel claims some mistake in bills
1:05P	Phone rings 2 times - Possibly answered in some other part of house.
1:06P	Hodel on phone - "I just got back yesterday - It's 65 miles across the border from Arizona - Sonita (?) Fishing is

good. Talked to Dr. Ignacia Renal (?) much interested in making a sanitroium out of the place. Cost 1,000,000 pesos to build. I'd just as soon lease it. Are you a Mexican citizen? Your'e not. I got some photos. Come on over and talk about it. Another Dr., an associate of mi went downthere today to look at it. Would clean about 5000.00 a month. When you come in from Upland the next time, bring her with you so I can meet. Upland 024277 is h phone number. She is a nurse.

1:16P   Phone rings - Hodel answers - caught 27 sea bass - may go down next weekend. Talks about his trip. Fine climate, etc.

1:20P   Hodel starts typing.

1:22P   Phone rings. Hodel answers, "Yes father. I was in Mexico trying to work up a business down there. There have been some new developmnts that I want to tell you about. OK, Dad, I'll be seeing you.

1:26P   Hodel dials phone, mail me my slip for my deposits last month.

1:29P   Phone rings - Hodel answers. Oh Joe (?) "They're working on your phone right now. How soon can she come over. I'll wait for her. I'll be glad to have her in here. Does she do day work? How much do you pay her. Oh, she's just a friend.

1:56P   Phone rings - Hodel answers. Talks about repairs to garage

2:04P   Phone rings - Hodel answers "Pretty good, Pat. I'm just going out - can you be here in 45 minutes. Maybe tomorrow then.

2:05P   Hodel dials - Inspector 372 - Mr. Landy (?) No - I'll call him back.

2:06P	Hodel dials – no conversation.
2:07P	Hodel dials – Is Dr. Barrett there. This is Dr. Hodel. I just got back from Mexico. I went on a fishing trip. We drove down. I notice we got no business on the Research Maybe on account of phone disconnections. Discusses efforts to build up Laboratories business.
2:15P	Hodel dials – no conversation.
2:20P	Phone rings – Hodel answers – unable to make out conversation.
2:25P	Hodel dials – Asks for Mr. Rockey – 2All the letter does is to confirm that he is an independent contractor. Relative to unemployment payment to someone.
3:00P	Talking to some woman. She said something about doing some work for Hodel. Took her to some other part of house.
3:02P	Hodel starts typing.
3:15P	Hodel dials phone "Is Mr. Ed Wilcox there". Something about Ed Being able to receive a message from Tibet. "I'm expecting a message from Mr. ? of Tibet. (Ed is apparently a ham short-waver)
3:20P	Hodel dials phone – no answer.
3:28P	Phone rings – Hodel answers. "Hello, dear. How are the children. Did you find your suit-case? I'd love to come down but I can't get away from here. Can't you come in. Try and do it.
3:34P	Hodel – "Will you see if PR 8086 is actually busy"? Hodel has been trying to reach this number ever since he
3:45P	talked to Ed Wilcox. I believe it is the phone number of another ham.
4:00P	Morgan, D.A.'s office, on duty.

	5:10P	Telephone rang - no answer
	6:35P	Telephone rang - no answer
	8:00P	Meyer, LAPD on duty. some one moving around.
	9:20P	Phone rang 6 timex - didn't hear anyone answer.
	9:55P	People moving around making lot of noise.
	10:05P	Some girls around talking - phone rang - no one answered. Hodel don't seem to be around.
	10:13P	Phone rang 35 times - girls still around - no answer.
	10:23P	Hodel enters - says he is tired - says something about getting something to eat - all go out to kitchen.
	11:00P	Hodel and girls go out to eat.
	11:20P	Phone rang - no answer.
3-16-50	12:30A	Hodel and girls return.
	1:00A	Girls talking about having babys and how to keep from having them
	2:00A	Wean, LAPD, on duty. Several women talking.
	2:30A	Some women leave - Hodel now talking with two women. Radio playing too loud to hear.
	3:15A	One woman leaves.
	3:30A	Hodel apparently gone to bed. All quiet.
	8:00A	Phone rings twice. Hodel answers - a patient with a sore said he would come see him today.
	8:00A	Egger, D.A.'s office on duty
	8:30A	All quiet.
	9:00A	All quiet.
	9:00A	Can hear snoring - apparently hodel.
	9:30A	All quiet.
	10:00A	All quiet.
	10:30A	All quiet.

HODEL FILE - ~~107~~ /26

127

	11:00A	All quiet.
	11:25A	Phone rings - Hodel answers talking about Mexico. Apparently with some woman - says he will meet her at 3 PM today.
	11:30A	Hodel moving around
	11:45A	Hodel still moving around - some bathroom noises
	11:55A	Hodel still moving around
3-17-50	12:15P	Some desk noises - Hodel leaves room Snyder, D.A.'s office on duty.
	12:55P	Hodel calls Sears-Roebuck on Santa Monica Blvd. in regards to mattress covers. Who knows, might be a sale, eh? Also calls Broadway-Hollywood-same subject.
	2:10P	Hodel typing, and mumbling to himself.
	2:45P	Still noise of typing, among various and sundry other noises.
	3:30P	Phone rings 5 times - no answer
	3:50P	Female voice in distance - unintelligible.
	4:00P	Phone rings - Hodel answers - some chatter regarding personal loans - also some ta k about someone having personal cards printed - talks by selling tea wholesale. $12. per#retail- 40% off - 2% ten days
	4:10P	Phone rings - Hodel answers - someone coming right over Snyder off duty 4:15PM

HODEL FILE - ~~108~~ /っ フ
3-16-50
SPOOL 37

128

	4:20P	Hodel dials Rompage Hardware Store on Hollywood Blvd. about some delivery.
	4:35P	Someone called at suggestion of Ed Wilcox - conversation pertaining to Ham station W6CNB (CMB?)
36	5:05P	Some man, woman and a little boy arrived - adults discuss the CPS
	6:03P	Hodel answerd the phone and promised to be right over.
	6:10P	Hodel makes call to OL 5851 - couldn't get his party. Dials another number - "Hello Mabel - is Erwin there?" Talk about sending Erwin a check (Erwin Hough) for digging some thing.
	7:44P	Examination of a woman patient, who is coming back Tuesday.
	7:50P	Hodel is typing.
	8:00P	Meyer, LAPD, on duty. Hodel dials phone - asks operator OL 5851 - no answer - hangs up.
	8:45P	Hodel left - all quiet.
	9:18P	Phone rang 6 times - no answer.
	11:00P	Phone rang 8 times - no answer.
	11:40P	Phone rang 5 times - no answer.
	2:00A	Hodel apparently sleeping. Can hear snoring.
	8:00A	J. McGrath - D.A.'s office on duty
	9:30A	No activity
	11:00A	Hodel up
	12:30A	Around bathroom
	12:00noon	Egger, D.A.'s office on duty
	12:30P	Hodel moving around room.
	1:00P	Hodel made phone call regarding sewage disposal or some digging on his property. Hodel said that he was in a hurry to get the work done, and he would wait for the workmen this afternoon.

HODEL FILE - ~~109~~ *128*

129

	1:15P	Hodel moving around. Phone rings 3 times, must have been answered other room.
	1:20P	Hodel out of room - can hear him talking to several men in background.
Re-corded 1 min to 36½	1:25P	Called <u>Miss White</u> about placing an ad in the paper - said th ad is in the name of E.L. Marsh in the categroy of furnishec rooms and apts. "Shang-ri-la" is at top of ad. Hodel wants to change ad to read; Artists and writers preferred.
	1:30P	Hodel typing at desk.
	1:45P	Hodel leaves room.
	2:10P	Can hear some machine noises - sounds like an electric hand drill. No conversation, drill keeps going on and off.
	2:20P	All quiet.
	2:35P	Phone rings 4 times - no answer.
	2:45P	Machine noise - off - whistling in background - some moving around.
	2:50P	Can hear talking, two or three men in background, sound lik they might be in basement; cannot make out conversation.
	3:00P	Can still hear muffled conversation with occasional machine noises; sawing, etc.
	3:30P	Hodel or someone moving about desk - same background noises men and machines working
	3:45P	Same as above
	4:00P	Still some background noises as stated above.
	4:15P	Same as above
	4:20P	Phone rings 6 timex - no answer - can hear walking around however.
	4:25P	Hodel called SY 94490 - asked for Fritz. Fritz not there.
	4:25P	Hronek, D.A.'s office on duty.

HODEL FILE - ~~110~~ /2-7 ¹³⁰

5:04P	Phone rings 7 times - no answer.
5:25P	Phone rings 5 times - no answer.
6:19P	Phone rings 1 time - must be answered in another room.
7:20P	Hodel returns and starts typing.
7:45P	Phone rings - Hodel answered - talked to someone about his trip to Mexico.
7:55P	Meyer, LAPD, on duty. All quiet.
7:57P	Hodel and some woman came in-talking in another room.
8:00P	Phone rings. Hodel answers - talking to someone who just got back from Frisco.
8:15P	Still talking to female who came in with him-can't make out what they are saying.
8:40P	Radio on - still talking.
8:45P	Hodel on phone - radio too loud to hear - said something about 1735 No. La Brea.
11:10P	The guy with the accent came in - radio on too loud - two women, one don't seem to understand English, other translates to her (mother and daughter)
11:25P	Hodel telling about his fishing in Mexico.
36-49½ 11:30P	Women leave - Hodel and man with accent - talking recorded - hard to hear. Hodel says probably they are watching me, talk about selling some of his stuff at an auction - says someone don't know anything to tell. Hodel said something about getting married again - talks about place in Mexico. Says it will clear about 4 or 5,000 a month. Hodel talking about Tibet and a letter he wrote there, says it is quite a job getting a letter sent there. Radio still on - talk world aff

HODEL FILE - 111 / 30
3-18-50

12:40A	Hodel - "Do you think those "Bastards" will try to bring action because I am renting rooms". Hodel says "Do you think we could hire some girl to find out what they are doing".
12:45A	Talking about women.
1:00A	Man with accent left - Hodel turned radio off - should have done that a hr. ago.
1:15A	Sounds like Hodel going to bed.
2:00A	Brechel, LAPD, on duty. All is quiet.
6:00A	Radio turned on (Sta KHJ) must have been left turned on as there was no one up to have turned it on. The program is first of the day.
6:20A	Radio still playing - Hodel still snoring.
7:30A	Radio still playing.
8:00A	J. McGrath, D.A.'s office on duty.
9:30A	No activity - radio now off.
10:30A	Phone rings - answered in rear of home.
11:45A	Phone rings 2 times - answered in rear.
12:50P	No sound
1:00P	Egger, D.A.'s office on duty.
1:15P	Seems to be moving around in other sections of the house, but otherwise All quiet.
1:25P	Hodel in background - conversation with woman.
2:00P	Woman's voice in background.
2:30P	Phone 1 time, but could hear no one answer - all quiet.
3:30P	All quiet.
3:45P	Background noises - Hodel and woman talking.
4:00P	Morgan, D.A.'s office, on duty
4:50P	Someone opened and closed all the drawers in the desk

HODEL FILE - ~~112~~ /3/   ¹³²
    4:00   MORGAN ON DUTY
    4:50P   (hurriedly) also sounds of paper shuffling and scrambling in

               another part of the room.

49½-50½ 4:55P   Telephone rang - Hodel answered - conversation regarding room

               rental - Hodel turned party down.

50½- 5:05P   Hodel telephoned - conversation regarding rental or room
54½

               wherein Hodel suggested that some part time work around place

               could be applied on Rental of rooms - made appointment for

               tomorrow about 11 AM to show place - Hodel leaving tonight at

               7 PM.

    5:13P   Telephone rang - no answer.

54½-55 5:20P   Telephone rang - Hodel "Yes, yes" What did you say your name

               is - Madeline Smith - Oh, suppose you call me tomorrow at

               12". Ends "Alright goodbye".

    5:23P   Hodel (I guess) dialed phone several times - no answer.

    5:30P   Going through drawers again - sounds of dog whining ~~forxix~~

               ~~itxwhinix~~ Typing noise.

55-55½ 5:32P   Hodel and woman (sounds like Mrs. Hodel) conversing about some

               medical term - Hodel "There's about a millionth of an ounce in

               the human body", etc. ~~xHodelxxxxxx~~

55½-56 6:12P   Hodel dialed phone - Hodel "What time does the owl show go on.

               What time does the whole show end?" Ends, "Thank you".

56½- 7:00P   Telephone rang - Hodel "She left/about ½ hour ago my place
56 3/4

               She should be there about now". Hope you can keep it under

               control". Ends "Goodbye".

   7:15P   Hodel conversing with another woman, who he called Gladys

               about some engravings they were looking at. They discussed h

               cursing sounded in French, Spanish, and Chinese.

HODEL FILE - ~~113 / 3~~   133

563/4- 7:43P 60	Telephone rang - Hodel "Hello Jill (or something) How's everything? Under control? Etc. Are you a tea lover? I have some tea for you - some very special tea - I am abou to take off for the evening now, etc. something about an eighteen year - answering the phone, etc.
8:00P	Wean, LAPD, on duty.
9:10P	Phone rang once, no one answered.
9:25P	Phone rang 3 times - no one answered.
9:50P	A man enters house, and asks for Hodel - some woman tells hi he is gone. He leaves.
10:55P	Hodel returns - phones andasks someone if they would like to hear some music. Says OK, and hangs up.
11:15P	Hodel talking with eighteen year old girl - radio too loud to understand.
11:40P	Hodel typing.

3-19-50

2:00A	Brechel, LAPD, on duty. All is quiet except Hodel is snorin
9:30A	Jamison, D.A.'s office - all quiet.
10:00A	voices - not distinguishable.
11:20A	All quiet.
11:30A	Tapping sound.
11:55A	Hodel - in bathroom - flushes toilet.
11:58A	Hodel takes a bath - says "poor fish".
12:00noon	Egger, D.A.'s office on duty.
12:15P	Hodel walking around desk noises.
12:20P	Hodel turns on the symphony on radio.
1:00P	Symphony still on - no other noise.
1:30P	Symphony still on; can hear Hodel talking to woman in background.

HODEL FILE - ~~114~~ / 3 3

134

1:45P	Hodel answers door bell, lets in woman - he talks to her abou renting her a room in return he will knock off the rent - an work she does for him such as cleaning and taking care of his quarters. Negro woman has her minor daughter with her.
1:50P	Phone rings - Hodel says "Mrs Hodel is out - I can take message. He said he is going down to the beack about 4 PM today - talks about renting room.
2:00P	Hodel again talking to negro woman. Hodel asks her daughter where she goes to school - the girl says-a catholic school.
2:10P	Colored woman and child leaving. woman is going to think it over - about renting room. Woman then starts talking about Doctor's-Hodel tells her about his clinic at 1st and Central Woman said she had a curettemat (curettement ?) in 1944. Hodel said he has done lots of them. Hodel and woman continue to talk about doctors, sickness, and other medical subjects. (Hodel seems to be acting overly nice to this woma He must be trying to talk her into renting the room, or ?) Hodel tells her that Dr. Hill, a colored Doctor, lives next door.
2:30P	Woman leaves
2:50P	Phone rings 2 times, must have bean answered in another room Hodel moving about desk.
3:15P	Hodel leaves room - all quiet.
3:45P	All quiet.
SPOOL 38 4:00P	Hronek, D.A.'s office, on duty.

HODEL FILE - ~~115~~/34

135

O	5:00P	Sounds like someone uses the vacuum cleaner.
	6:00P	No sound
	7:00P	No sound
	8:00P	No sound. Wean, LAPD, on duty
		Woman's voice in background.
	10:30P	Phone rings 3 times, can't hear anyone answer.
	11:00P	All quiet.

3-20-50

	12:30P	Hodel typing.
	2:00A	Brechel, LAPD, on duty
0-1	2:08A	Phone rings. Hodel answers "Hello. hes yes". Short conversation is recorded. Apparently is receiving instructions, and agrees to it. "Yes, I'll do it", or "Yes, I'll be there". Hodel was in bedroom when he received call and must have been waiting for it as phone rang once only.
	2:09R	Hodel went out of room after the call.
	2:48A	Hodel returns to room.
	3:25A	Hodel moving around room.
	3:45A	All quiet.
	8:00A	J. McGrath, D.A.'s office on duty
	9:30A	All quiet, no activity.
	10:15A	Phone call received - can't hear-too much racket - Hodel has dinner engagement tonight. Going out of town Wednesday. Hodel talking about selling the house.
	10:17A	Hodel makes phone call - too much static to hear.
	10:21A	Hodel makes phone call - cannot hear.
	10:23A	Phone call received - lots of static
	11:54A	Phone call received by Hodel - talks low - can't hear.
	11:55A	Hodel makes phone call - can't make out.

HODEL FILE - ~~116~~ /3 J   136

12:00noon	Snyder, D.A.'s office on duty
1:10P	Phone rings - inquiry regarding rooms or house - Hodel tells her to call back between 3:30 and 4:00. Says he is going out for afternoon.
1:15P	Hodel call UCLA - seeking information re. Burrel Ives. ~~Reserves 2 seats, 13th row, near aisle - did not get date.~~
1:50P	The doctor Hodel is taking a bath.
2:15P	Hodel leaves house.
2:50P	Phone rings 8 times - no answer.
4:00P	Hronek, D.A.'s office on duty.
6:55P	Two women and a man carry on a conversation about books and poetry - the fellow is apparently an actor - talks about himself mile a minute.
7:05P	Moved to another part of house - conversation unintelligible.
8:00P	Meyer, LAPD, on duty. Hear people talking, but unable to understand.
8:40P	Man and woman talking, not English, can't understand.
9:00P	Hodel talking to some man with an accent (not same) sounds like a photographer talking about taking pictures. Hodel shows some pictures he took.
9:12P	Radio on - not Hodel's music.
10?00P	Still playing Chinese - music worse then Hodel's music.
10:25P	Sounds like Hodel around by himself - radio off.
10:50P	Hodel and some guy with accent talking, and looking at map of Mexico. (The photographer).
11:05P	Talking about going (to Mexico) want to leave tomorrow night, Hodel says don't tell anyone. Hodel says He has to be back Wednesday. He is going to Santa Barbara, and won't be back until Sunday. Sounds like they are going totake pictures Sounds like Hodel is trying to pull a fast one of some kind

HODEL FILE - ~~117~~ / 3 6

	11:05P	This other guy seems to know the country.
	11:25P	Guy with accent leaves, says will call tomorrow and make arrangements about going if they go
	11:30P	Hodel moving around by himself
3-21-50	12:00A	Sounds like Hodel has ~~gone to bed~~ - ~~all~~ quiet.
	2:00A	Brechel, LAPD, on duty. All is quiet. Hodel must have slep in another part of house. There were no snoring noises all morning. Music in the background all morning till 6:30A coming from rear part of house.
	8:00A	J. McGrath, D.A.'s office on duty
	8:45A	Phone call received - could not hear in back room
	8:57A	Phone call received - ~~knkk~~ can't make out - ended conversation at 9:22 - could not hear anything-too much noise and static.
	9:25A	Hodel made phone call - hard to hear - said something about fishing - also a test on a patient named Momas.
	9:35A	Insurance inspector calls to inspect some belongings of one of the tenants.
	9:40A	Hodel makes phone call to some doctor - sounds like Barrymore
	10:45A	Phone call received for someone else - Hodel said "I will have her call you".
	10:47A	Someone phoned - Hodel said "I will get hold of you as soon as the stuff is here."
	10:55A	Hodel phones someone about $50.00 a month he paid some woman "Said I'm in trouble" want some advice - do you have a farm.
	11:00A	Phone call received - Hodel ran to back of house-answered could not hear.

HODEL FILE – 119 /38   138

12:40P	Hodel dials – "Is this Miss Mathis?" How is Dr. Nicholas? Shall I write him? I'll write him?
12:42P	Hodel is typing and hence conversation unintelligible.
12:47P	Hodel dials (Tu 4826) Asks for medical desk.
1:00 to 1:15P	Hodel and Dorothy engage in a little loving
1:16P	Water running
1:20P	Hodel typing
1:55P	Dorothy dials phones Asks for ? This is Mrs Rogel (?) Tell him I called.
1:56P	Hodel dials – Water running – conversation unintelligible. He's talking about a job. "I prefer part time. Is it hospit or clinic. What pay is he offering. Talks about his work as chief of staff at clinic. I'm medical director of a local laboratory, but I have too much time. Send me your contract form.
2:02P	Talking about their children.
2:10P	Phone rings. Hodel answers "I'll call you this evening about 7 or 8 o'clock. Maybe we'll go tomorrow Joe".
2:35P	Quiet.
2:55P	Phone rings 6 times – no one answers.
4:00P	Still quiet.
4:05P	Hronek D.A.'s office on duty
4:33P	Phone rang 15 times – no answer
4:45P	" " 10 times – no answer
6:52P	" " 4 times – no answer
7:40P	" " 6 times – no answer
8:00P	Meyer, LAPD, on duty. All quiet.
9:20P	Phone rang 3 times, didn't hear anyone answer.

HODEL FILE - 118 / 3 >

11:01A	Hodel makes phone call to some one.
11:05A	A woman comes to see Hodel - sounds like Dorothy-they go to rear of the house - can't hear.
11:45A	Sullivan, D.A.'s office on duty. Can hear Hodel and woman talking but unable to understand as they are in some other part of house.
11:55A	Hodel typing
12:05P	Dorothy asks Hodel for telephone number - he gives her HO 93311 - Albert Van. She apparently called from some other part of house.
12:12P	Dorothy Hodel dials phone - asks for Mr. Holser (Said she was Dorothy Hodel) No conversation.
12:14P	Dorothy dials phone - asks for Rollin Brown - talks to him "I went down to Mexico and had a nice time fishing, that's why I haven't seen you. Fell off the pier. Told him he should have picked up some of the weights we had dropped down there. Talks about meeting Doctor in Mexico and about the place in Mexico. Talks about how George and he fly down ther It's in Sonora County. It's near Otho (?) About 400 miles from here (George is prompting her) There are whore houses there, and we visited one. George was seeing rashes all over the place (She's sure giving this guy a sales talk) Hodel is typing and hence unable to hear Dorothy's conversation.
12:26P	Dorothy finished conversation.
12:27P	Dorothy dials phone - HO 93311 charged to HO 98485 - Dorothy dials phone - This Dorothy Huston. Is Mr. Bangs (?) there. Please have him call me at O1 3476, or Santa Monica 42421. George tells Dorothy John won't call her and won't

DEL FILE - 120

3-21-50

SPOOL 38

11:25 P	Sounds like Hodel just came home - at his desk moving papers.
11:40P	Phone rang - Hodel answers "Hello, Tracey - any calls for me?" That was all.
12:30A	Hodel snoring

3-22-50	2:00A	Brechel LAPD on duty - All is quiet
	7:25A	Sounds like Hodel getting up - running water in bathroom
	8:00A	M. McGrath, D.A.'s office on duty
	8:30 a	All quiet
	10:40A	Phone rings 6 times - no answer
	12:00P	Sullivan, D.A.'s office on duty
	12:00P-4:00P	Bimson, Belle, and Sullivan listening to past recordings as Hodel has been out for the entire day.
	4:00P	Egger, D.A.'s office on duty . Hodel still out.
	5:00P	No noise-Hodel still out
	5:06P	Woman enters, but not Hodel
	5:05P	Phone rings 10 times - no answer
	6:00P	All quiet.
	6:10P	Hodel comes in - works at desk
	6:30P	Can hear Hodel and Woman talking in background - Hodel still working around desk.
	6:35P	Hodel phoning, sayd "This is Dr. Hodel returning your call". Too much background and line noise to make out most of conversation - something about records. Also talking about urine specimens and venerial disease. other party seems to be doing most of the talking. Conversation is along medical lines.

HODEL FILE - 121   141

	6:45P	Woman comes in and calls "Doctor" Hodel is still on phone, can hear the woman walking around, humming, then leaves.
	6:50p	Hodel still on phone (not talking much).
	7:00P	Conversation has now turned to corporations, stocks, and bonds with Hodel doing very little talking.
	7:20P	Conversation over - Hodel moving around desk.
	7:30P	Hodel still moving around desk.
	7:55P	Hodel still at desk - no conversation. Hodel leaves room - then comes back.
	8:00P	Meyer, LAPD, on duty. All quiet.
	8:22P	Hodel and some girl come in - talking - can't understand too much other noise.
	8:35P	Radio on.
	9:40P	Hodel by himself - typing.
	10:30P	All quiet except radio on.
	10:45P	Radio off - all quiet.
3-23-50	2:00A	Brechel, LAPD, on duty. All quiet.
	3:00A	Hodel makes visit to lavatory, returns to bed.
	8:00A	J. McGrath, D.A.'s office on duty
	10:15A	All quiet.
	12:00noon	All quiet.

HODEL FILE - 122   142

3-23-50

4:00P-8:00P Hronek, D.A.'s office, on duty

	4:10P	Occasional movement in the background
	4:30P	All quiet
	5:00P	All quiet
	5:20P	All quiet
	6:00P	All quiet
	6:30P	All quiet
O-	7:00P	Hodel comes in and makes a call - about some compound takes the address, 60E 42nd St., New York 17, N.Y. "I'm writing myself". Series of yea, yea, yea, alright, yea, yea, that's from the U.S. Chemical News - USI Chem News, Feb 1950 - I know, yea, yea, they have written - OK thanks, Good night.
	7:15P	Phone rang 5 times - no answer.
	7:35P	Door bell rang - some woman comes in - conversation in the background.
O-6	7:45P	Hodel came in with Dorothy - phone rang (recorded)
	8:00P	Meyer, LAPD, on duty. Radio on.
	8:02P	Phone rang - Hodel answers - said Exbrook 32473, about a phone number.
	9:30P	Radio turned on - don't hear anyone.
	10:30P	Some woman just came in - Hodel asks if she ever saw a certain book - talking about "Matches" (The woman is) Sounds like she designs match covers.
	11:20P	The dame is still talking, boy she is sure wound up.

HODEL FILE - 123
3-24-50

12:15A	Woman left, had been talking since 10:30P
12:40A	Dame back again and still talking
12:45A	Dame left again.
12:55A	Hodel typing - radio off
1:15A	Hodel called and sent a nite letter to a Mrs. Barbe 1543 Valejo St., San Francisco. Something about birthday wishes. Message read "My birthday wishes must go to you. I hope each year will make -------?-----? Am doing my best and will continue trying. Please leave me know how things are going".
2:00A	Brechel, LAPD, on duty. Hodel typing.
2:10A	Typing stops - goes to lavatory - urinates then all quiet.
2:15A	To bed - all quiet.
8:00A	J. McGrath, D.A.'s office on duty
9:45A	All quiet.
10:10A	Phone call received. Hodel answers - says "Oh yes, fine yea, yea. Well, all right, that's good , as soon as you know, yeah, good," Hangs up.
10:50A	Phone rings 2 times - answered in rear of house.
10:52A	Hodel typing at his desk.
11:30A	Phone call received - Hodel answers - for someone else.
12:20P	Phone call received by Hodel "Yeah, yeah, oh that's swell. Yeah, yeah, oh that's good, uh huh. He will give you some good advice anyway -" Talking about a $1000.00 order now. of some kind. Interested in a merger - "all right Tom, goodbye".

26	5 to 9 talk of trial
	9 to 40 much talk of juggling figures.
27	13 to 15 - talk about deducting some money as repayment of loans to father and son.
	18 to 22 - wire bad Skip - listen from 40 on to
	46 to 48 - very interesting (cut this spool off at 50 the end is loose).

Spool #37

3-5	Conversation regarding tax case and Dahlia
5-17	Conversation regarding code and mailing - have to be careful - income tax starts at 15 on Spool 25

HODEL FILE - 125   145

3-24-50

	4:00P	Hronek, D.A.'s office on duty--All quiet.
	4:30P	Hodel starts typing.
6-8½	5:00P	Call out by Taylor MU 2165, one of Hodel's associates.
8½-11	5:10P	Same person making a call and talking
	6:18P	Hodel starts typing again
11	6:41P	Hodel comes in with another guy -"sit down, let me fix us a drink -" They talk about foods and drinks of different nations - girl comes in. Hodel call Churchill 92146.
	8:00P	Meyer, LAPD, on duty. All quiet.
	8:40P	Phone rang 4 times - too much background noise - coudn't hear anyone answer.
	9:50P	Hodel comes in with some man, talking about Mexico - lots of moise in background.
11-19	10:20P	Radio on playing records - some girl around
nothing	11:15P	Radio off - Hodel xxxxxxtalking to man, hard to hear.
	11:18P	Phone rang - Hodel answers - sounded like talking to someone in other part of house - man left.
	11:50P	Hodel comes back in - starts typing
3-25	12:05A	Radio on again.
19-20	12:30A	Phone - kHodel answers - radio on - said something about having money by then.
	12:36A	Radio off - sounded like Hodel left.
	1:00A	Wean, LAPD, on duty. Someone moving around and typing
	1:30A	Hodel returns.
	2:00A	All quiet - not sure if Hodel left or is in bed
	3:30A	Phone rings 3 times - woman calls Hodel - no more conversation.
	4:30A	All quiet.

HODEL FILE - 126   146

     8:00P   Meyer, LAPD, on duty. All qiet.

20-61 11:10P   Hodel and Baron (man with accent) came in talking low -
     can't hear (recording) only stays few minutes and leaves.
     I was wrong - was in bathroom. Sounded like Hodel said
     something about Black Daliah. Baron said something about
     F.B.I. Then talked about Tibet - sounded like Hodel wants
     to get out of the country. mentioned passport - Hodel
     giving Baron dope on how to write to Tibet. Hodel talking
     about Mexico - going down and take pictures and write a
     story. Hodel seems afraid about something. Hodel says
     his Sanatarium - if he got it started in Mexico - would be
     "Safe".

Spool 39

     12:00A   Spool ran out - changing - talking about women.
Mar 26,1950
0-50 12:07A   Not much talk - still recording. Hodel says he wants money
     and power - talking about China - talking about selling
     some of Hodel's paintings or something. Hodel talking
     about picture police have of him and some girl - thought
     he had destroyed them all - wire quit at 50 - new one going
     on - not much talk.

Spool 40
3-37 1:00A   Had trouble with one spool. Had to use another - still
     talking about selling paintings.

     1:50A   Sounds like Baron left - don't know if there is anything
     on these records or not.

     2:00A   Hodel at his desk - all else quiet - Good night.

     3:00P   Hodel having party - about 8 people - party ends - someone

     3:30P   listening to radio programs. Wean, LAPD, on duty.

     5:00P   Woman and Hodel talking, but radio too loud to hear.

146

HODEL FILE - 127

37-49	6:20P	Hodel talking with woman
	6:35P	Recorded
49-50½	8:00P	Phone - Hodel answers - recorded - couldn't hear too well. Meyer, LAPD, on duty.
50½-60	10:55P	Hodel and some man came in - not sure if Baron or not - guess it is (recording) talking about paintings and etc. And Asia - Change records

Spool 41

0-1½	11:15P	New wire on-guess both left.
1½-23	11:55P	Hodel-some woman come in - also the Baron. Hodel and Baron talking low - guess woman left. Woman back. Guess same gabby woman that was there other nite. About matches Advertising woman left again. Gabbey is back - all looking at pictures and etc.
3-27	1:00A	Everyone left.
	2:00A	All quiet. Good nite.

D.A. Lt. Jemison—Dorothy Huston Hodel Interview

DA TRANSCRIPTS- DOROTHY HODEL INTERVIEW 3/22/1950

Bk 29
Pg 14

STATEMENT OF DOROTHY HARVEY HODEL TAKEN AT 410 SANTA MONICA
PIER, SANTA MONICA BY LT. FRANK B. JEMISON AT 12:15 P. M.
ON MARCH 22, 1950.

File No.

Charge: Murder

Title:

Deputy:

Present:

Questions by: Lt. Jemison

Reported by: Dora A. Parisho

Q What is your full name?
A Dorothy Harvey Hodel.

Q What is your residence address at the present time?
A 410 Santa Monica Pier.

Q What is your phone number here?
A I don't have a phone. There is a fishing renting place
downstairs, SM 42421.

Q What is your present occupation?
A Housewife. I do a little writing, but I'm not working
at the present time.

Q Were you formerly married to Dr. George Hodel?
A Yes.

Q Are you now divorced from him?
A Yes.

Q How long have you been divorced from him?
A The interlocutory decree was in 1944 and the final was
in 1945.

Q Do you have any children from him?
A Yes, I have three boys.

Q Are you acquainted with Tamara Hodel?
A Yes.

Q And is Dr. George Hodel the father of Tamara?
A Yes.

Q Are you acquainted with her mother?
A Yes.

Q What is her name?
A Dorothy.

MAR 23 1950

-1-

Q Where is she living now, what city?
A I believe San Francisco, but I'm not sure.

Q You are familiar, are you with the trial that Dr. Hodel just went through in connection with Tamara?
A I kno w about it, but I didn't attend it.

Q Do you know Lillian Lenorak?
A Yes, I do.

Q When did you first become acquainted with her, about what year?
A I think it was about 1940. Let me see, say '46. I'm not really sure.

Q When did you last see her?
A Just before she went to Camarillo and just before her mother came for her. Anyway, after shw was ill over there at George's.

Q Do you know her mother?
A No.

Q When you last saw her did you feel she was a mental case, is that what your information is?
A I felt she must be. The little boy was running around and was very distressed. Poor little kid.

Q I will now show you a photograph of Beth Short, Santa Barbara No. 11419 and ask you whether or not you have ever seen that young lady in your life?
A No, I never have.

Q Did you have a conversation with Dr. Hodel about the murder of Beth Short?
A No, unless we mentioned it when it was in the papers, but I don't like to read about things like that. I can't say for sure that I have never mentioned her name to him, but it may have been in passing.

Q Did he ever tell you, "They can't pin that murder on me?"
A No, to the best of my knowledge he didn't and doesn't know her.

Q On or about the date of her murder, January 15, 1947 do you remember being out until 4:00 in the morning with George Hodel and coming in slightly intoxicated? Now, that's three years ago.
Q A Well, I think I explained before we never went on drinking parties because I don't drink because of certain tendencies to drink too much and particularly if I were near

-2-

171

1 him I would not drink because from a medical point of view
2 he does not approve of my drinking and I don't know that I
   understood that question.

3 Q Well, the information that I have is that he was quite
   intoxicated himself and at that time on that occasion stated
4 that they couldn't pin the Black Dahlia murder on him.
   A No. No, that isn't true.
5

6 Q Do you remember ever telling Tamar that?
   A No.

7 Q Did you ever tell Tamar that Dr. George Hodel was out
   the night before the murder with Beth Short at a party?
8 A No, I was living at my brother's house at the time. We
   were not living at the same house. I wouldn't know what he was
9 doing.

10 Q What was your brother's address at that time?
   A 2121 Loma Vista Place.
11

   Q Has anybody ever told you that Dr. George Hodel had Beth
12 Short over to his home?
   A No.
13

   Q Nobody has ever told you that?
14 A No. No one has ever told me that.

15 Q For your information her photograph has been identified by
   certain persons as resembling the young lady that was over to
16 his house prior to the murder. You never heard anything about
   that?
17 A I never did.

18 Q As a matter of fact you are on quite a friendly relation
   aren't you, with Dr. George Hodel?
19 A We are friends.

20 Q And at the time of this murder, which was so publicized
   and made headlines in the newspaper at that time, weren't
21 you on pretty friendly terms with him?
   A We have always been on friendly terms.
22

   Q That was January 15, 1947 three years and two months
23 ago.
   A I'm trying to relate it to when he got back from China.
24 Was that before or after he got back from China?

25 Q It was sometime after he got back from China. It was
   at a time when Dr. George Hodel had a medical clinic on East
26 First Street, near Central Avenue.
   A He had the clinic for a long time before he left.

-3-

172

Q Let's go back to the time and do you remember at that time of Dr. Hodel having noon lunch or dinner at the Biltmore?
A No.

Q Did you ever have lunch with Dr. Hodel at the Biltmore?
A I imagine so.

Q Would you know it to be a fact that Dr. Hodel did eat lunch or dinner on occasion at the Biltmore?
A He has taken me to lunch there once or twice and we have had dinner there perhaps.

Q For your information we know of other women that have had lunch with him at the Biltmore Hotel and dinner.
A It's a central location.

Q There is further information that Dr. Hodel stayed at the Biltmore Hotel on a few occasions. Do you remember those?
A I believe when he was between apartments when they had that three-day law in effect, he stayed I believe. I'm not sure. I think the Biltmore was among them. He made a tour of the hotels and stayed three days in each while he was finding an apartment.

Q You understand that a very serious crime has been committed here and the District Attorney would not like it if you were to withhold any information in connection with a murder of this type and we would like to have you give us any and all information you may have in connection with this murder on this suspect George Hodel. If there is anything you have to tell us, tell us.
A I have nothing to tell you that would bear out any idea you may have that he did this. All I know is that he is not the sort of man that would psychologically be the kind to do it. He has a fine record as a doctor and is a dedicated man. He has never had a fashionable practice. He could have had. He is a man that really cares about medicine, not of earning money, but it is incredible to me that he should be in any way connected with it.

Q You know that Dr. Hodel has had practice with surgical tools?
A I know he has neverpracticed surgery. His branch of medicine is V. D. generally and Administrative Medicine.

Q I show you Sheriff's Photograph B 119364 and will ask you is you recognize that?
A Yes.

Q Who is that?
A Dr. George Hodel.

-4-

Q Now in view of the fact that the District Attorney's office
is interested in contacting all persons that might know something
about whether or not Dr. Hodel had anything to do with this
murder, I now show you a photograph of a nude girl and ask
you if you recognize who that girl is. In other words,
we want to know her name and where we can contact her?
A There is something familiar about her face. I think she may
have been some model or something.

Q Would you say she is a colored girl or half Indian, do you
know?
A No.

Q Would you know who the photographer might be in connection
with this picture?
A No.

Q I show you another photograph of the same girl with a
man. Do you recognize that man in that photograph?
A I would say that was Dr. Hodel.

Q Do you know the person who owns the cat that they are holding
between them?
A No, I don't.

Q Q In other words, I am sincerely interested in contacting
this girl for information.
A No, I don't know her. I have seen her face. I have seen
photographs that George has of her.

Q Would you have any idea where we could find her?
A No.

Q I show you the third picture. Dr. Hodel and the colored
girl. You still can't place any person that might know where
I can find her?
A No, I don't know. I can't think.

Q Did you ever hear Dr. Hodel say anything more about
the details of this murder of Beth Short about the body or
anything about it?
A No, I never heard him discuss it at all.

Q Well, if you look back on the events that took place
about the time of the murder, did you have any reason to
suspect that Dr. Hodel might have had something to do with it?
A None whatever.

Q Let me advise you that we do have information that he did
associate with Beth Short and as you know the last place she

-5-

174

1   was seen alive was at the Biltmore Hotel in the evening
    of January 9, 1947.
2   A I didn't know that.

3   Q You are positive at this time that you never met that girl?
    A Very very sure.

4
5   Q What is the name of your attorney?
    A Robert Butts.

6   Q And what is his address?
    A It's the Bank of America Building at Hollywood and Ivar.
7   I forget the number.

8   Q Did he advise you to give a statement to the District
    Attorney's office?
9   A Yes.

10 Q He did request however that you get a copy of the statement
    is that right?
11 A That's right.

12 Q And as I have stated before, that's something the District
    Attorney has never done in connection to giving copies to any
13 witnesses at any time.
    A I didn't know.

14

15   *   *   *

16

17

18

19

20

21

22

23

24

25

26   -6-

D.A. Surveillance Timeline February 15—March 27, 1950

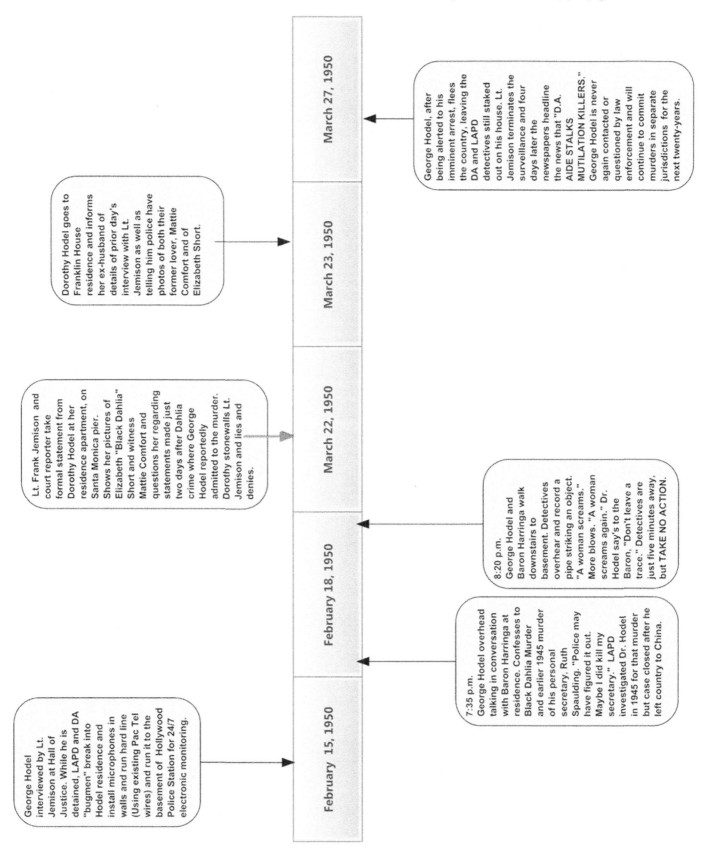

February 15, 1950

George Hodel interviewed by Lt. Jemison at Hall of Justice. While he is detained, LAPD and DA "bugmen" break into Hodel residence and install microphones in walls and run hard line (Using existing Pac Tel wires) and run it to the basement of Hollywood Police Station for 24/7 electronic monitoring.

February 18, 1950

7:35 p.m.
George Hodel overhead talking in conversation with Baron Harringa at residence. Confesses to Black Dahlia Murder and earlier 1945 murder of his personal secretary, Ruth Spaulding. "Police may have figured it out. Maybe I did kill my secretary." LAPD investigated Dr. Hodel in 1945 for that murder but case closed after he left country to China.

March 22, 1950

Lt. Frank Jemison and court reporter take formal statement from Dorothy Hodel at her residence apartment, on Santa Monica pier. Shows her pictures of Elizabeth "Black Dahlia" Short and witness Mattie Comfort and questions her regarding statements made just two days after Dahlia crime where George Hodel reportedly admitted to the murder. Dorothy stonewalls Lt. Jemison and lies and denies.

8:20 p.m.
George Hodel and Baron Harringa walk downstairs to basement. Detectives overhear and record a pipe striking an object. "A woman screams." More blows. "A woman screams again." Dr. Hodel say's to the Baron, "Don't leave a trace." Detectives are just five minutes away, but TAKE NO ACTION.

March 23, 1950

Dorothy Hodel goes to Franklin House residence and informs her ex-husband of prior day's details of interview with Lt. Jemison as well as telling him police have photos of both their former lover, Mattie Comfort and of Elizabeth Short.

March 27, 1950

George Hodel, after being alerted to his imminent arrest, flees the country, leaving the DA and LAPD detectives still staked out on his house. Lt. Jemison terminates the surveillance and four days later the newspapers headline the news that "D.A. AIDE STALKS MUTILATION KILLERS." George Hodel is never again contacted or questioned by law enforcement and will continue to commit murders in separate jurisdictions for the next twenty-years.

TEN STAR

Daily News

FINAL PEACH

Manchester Boddy, Publisher and Editor-in-Chief; Robert L. Smith, Associate Publisher and General Manager; Lee F. Payne, Executive Editor. Published daily except Sunday, 1257 S. Los Angeles Street, Los Angeles, (Calif.) Entered as 2nd class matter April 16, 1941 at connection Los Angeles Calif. under act of March 4, 1879 Carrier 1 fr 119 M.

SEVEN CENTS

LOS ANGELES 54   No. 17,233
FRI., MARCH 31, 1950

AN INDEPENDENT NEWSPAPER FOR INDEPENDENT PEOPLE

TEL. RICHMOND 6565

D. A. aide stalks mutilation killers

Dist. Atty. William E. Simpson said today one of his investigators is making "very good progress" in a renewed investigation of the unsolved mutilation murders of Jeanne French and Elizabeth Short, the Black Dahlia.

Simpson disclosed investigator Frank C. Jemison has been working several months on the cases,

independent of the Police department. Jemison was assigned to the task at the request of the 1949 County Grand jury.

The district attorney added his aide will continue with his inquiry "until he thinks he has sufficient evidence against a party or parties, and then will ask for formal murder complaints."

The bisected body of Elizabeth Short, 22, was found Jan. 15, 1947, in a vacant lot in the southwest sector.

Exactly one month later the body of Mrs. French, 45, obscenely marked with lipstick, was discovered in a field in West Los Angeles.

Chief of Detectives Thad Brown, meanwhile, discounted reports that vital evidence in the French slaying, in the form of blood-stained clothing, had disappeared from the West Los Angeles detective bureau.

Brown said the clothing, belonging to a short-lived suspect in the case, never was recorded as evidence because its owner was absolved of any connection with the crime two weeks after it occurred.

——CHECK CLASSIFIED AD——

Daily News 3/31/50

DA Investigators Jemison & Morgan

(Originally printed as Chapter 9 in Black Dahlia Avenger II, *Thoughtprint Press, 2012)*

Lt. Frank Jemison

ONE OF THE FEW MEN IN THE BLACK DAHLIA INVESTIGATION who it can be said was actually wearing a white hat was Lt. Frank B. Jemison of the Los Angeles District Attorney's Bureau of Investigation.

From everything that I've seen, he did his job, solved the case, and was just about to make the arrest when the powers that be pulled his plug. We can speculate all day about why. The reasons are many and varied.

However, what is not in dispute is The Order. Lt. Jemison, in his final closing report, made it crystal clear that he had been removed from the case [later independently confirmed in a 2004 television interview of DA investigator Walter Morgan] and ordered to hand over his investigation, interviews, and all his evidence, which included the wire recordings and transcripts, directly to LAPD Chief Thad Brown.

As I said in an earlier chapter, Lt. Jemison's saving grace was to copy his original investigation, complete with the Hodel-Black Dahlia File, and secure it in the DA's vault, where it would remain hidden for the next fifty-three years until finally being opened and revealed.

Los Angeles Hall of Justice, 210 W. Temple Street, Los Angeles

The above photo taken by the author in 2008 shows the downtown Los Angeles Hall of Justice at the corner of Temple and Broadway Streets. The HoJ built in 1925, has a long, colorful, and macabre history. Most of L.A.'s famous trials were held in this courthouse. The building served as a jail detention facility for prisoners awaiting trial, as well as housing the L.A. County Sheriff's Department, Coroner and District Attorney, including Lt. Jemison's office in the Bureau of Investigation.

The HoJ was within easy walking distance of all three of Dr. George Hodel's medical facilities: Health Department in Chinatown, First Street VD Clinic at First and Central, and his private medical office at Seventh and Flower Street.

The building has direct connections to our investigation.

1) In the early 1940s, Dr. George Hill Hodel's Health Department office was inside this building [1938-1942];

2) In 1947, the autopsy on Elizabeth "Black Dahlia" Short was performed in the Coroner's morgue in the basement of the HoJ, and the inquest into her death was held in a courtroom of the building; and

3) In 1949, Dr. George Hodel was arrested and booked into the jail facility here and was later tried in Superior Court on the lower floors of the premise. On February 15, 1950, George Hodel was detained and questioned by Lt. Jemison here, while at the same time, LAPD and DA sound technicians and detectives broke into the Franklin house to install the microphones.

Dr. Hodel was free to go only after Lt. Jemison got the "all clear" call from detectives as they exited the Franklin house, having "wired it for sound."

Charles Manson and the rest of his "Family" were tried and convicted here. So were RFK assassin Sirhan Sirhan, mobsters Bugsy Siegel and Mickey Cohen, actor Robert Mitchum, as well as most of L.A.'s historic bad boys and *femme fatales*. In addition to Elizabeth Short, this was also the morgue where the autopsies on Marilyn Monroe and Robert Kennedy were performed.

The building was deemed "unsafe" after the 1994 Northridge earthquake and has been vacant for nearly two decades. With such a distinguished history, hopefully, it will be saved from the wrecking ball, updated to current codes and preserved.

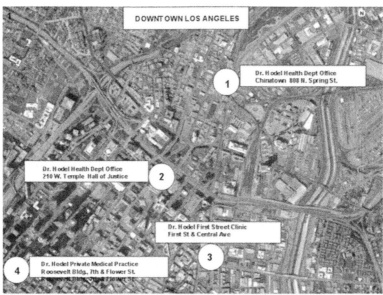

Dr. George Hill Hodel's four downtown L.A. medical office locations:
(1) Health Dept. Chinatown; (2) Health Dept., Hall of Justice [1938-1940];
(3) His privately owned, First Street VD Clinic; and (4) His private practice at Roosevelt Bldg.

Upper Left: GHH Chinatown office; Upper Right: First Street Clinic
Bottom: Dr. Hodel's private practice on 12th floor at Seventh and Flower

A FAMILY SECRET

"The Dahlia murder suspect was a doctor and we know who did it, but we couldn't put him away." —Lt. Frank Jemison Hall of Justice Summer, 1951

In mid-October 2006, I was contacted by a close surviving relative of District Attorney investigator, Lt. Frank B. Jemison. For privacy's sake, I will simply use his initials, "J.F." He advised me that he was Jemison's nephew [Jemison's sister's son], a medical doctor, and a retired Air Force colonel. Here in his own words is his description of his Uncle Frank, and one very important meeting he remembers from 1951:

Family background:
Frank was my mother's brother, the only son of a Methodist minister. He seemed a little eccentric to me. Every two years, he and his wife would fly to Detroit, pick up a new Cadillac, and drive through Ohio unannounced to visit his three sisters. If they weren't home—too bad, until two years later. He had not followed his father Dave's advice and entered the ministry and after graduation from Ohio Wesleyan College, he took off for the west coast. I thought he had a Law degree. Family rumor has it that he earned a good bit of money in real estate and as a financial advisor prior to his career as a DA investigator.

I know he was proud of his fortune, which was, at least in 1951, over one million dollars. While there was some family friction with Uncle Frank, he was always described as a person of impeccable personal integrity. I surmise that this integrity plus the fact that he had already made his fortune made him an excellent choice as investigator in the midst of apparent corruption. At his wife's death, the estate was left to Ohio Wesleyan.

The Black Dahlia Murder Case:
When I was 12 years old in the summer of 1951, I accompanied my family to a medical convention in San Francisco and we stopped in L.A. for three days, my only extended contact with Uncle Frank. At dinner, he asked if my father, a family physician, and I would like to see where he worked. At that time, the Hall of Justice was one of the, if not the, tallest buildings in LA. My father and Uncle Frank sat in the front seat and I sat in back. As they drove, Dad turned and said, "You know your Uncle Frank was the investigator for the Black Dahlia case." I liked the name but it didn't mean much to me. They explained that it was a famous murder case. I didn't listen too hard to the conversation until they said the body was cut up. Then I was all ears. Uncle Frank described the cuts, etc., and asked Dad what he thought. My father said he thought it had to be the work of a surgeon. Uncle Frank agreed and said that "We know who did it but we didn't have enough to put him away." For some reason, my twelve year old mind couldn't understand that. I wondered why, if they knew who did it they couldn't arrest him. I never thought of that case from that time, but the name "Black Dahlia" remained stuck in my mind. Just thought this might be interesting to you as background information. Really have enjoyed your book!

Sincerely Yours,
J.F. M.D. COL USAF (ret)

Dr. J.F.'s "background information" is much more than interesting. With what we already know, his family reflections are extremely illuminating, especially because of his certainty as to when Uncle Frank met with him and made these statements. It was the summer of 1951!

Let's briefly review Lt. Jemison's investigative chronology:

1) **October 1949**—Grand Jury appointed Lt. Frank Jemison to take over the Black Dahlia and other L.A. Lone Woman murder investigations. George Hill Hodel became DA Lt. Jemison's prime Dahlia suspect.

2) **February 15-March 27,** 1950—Jemison established an eighteen-man task force assigned to twenty-four-hour electronic-surveillance of Dr. Hodel's Franklin house.

3) **March 28, 1950**—George Hodel was tipped about surveillance. Realizing he was about to be arrested, he fled the residence. DA Lt. Jemison forced to remove surveillance equipment and shut down operation. After that, Lt. Jemison and police never again have contact with prime suspect, Dr. George Hill Hodel.

4) **February 1951**—Lt. Jemison ordered to close Dahlia case and turn all investigation and evidence and Hodel surveillance recordings and interviews over to LAPD. He complies, but locks away a "second set of investigative files" in the DA vault, where they remain untouched and unexamined until 2003.

5) **July 1951**—Lt. Jemison brought his vacationing brother-in-law, a medical doctor, and his twelve-year-old nephew, "J.F." to his office at the downtown Los Angeles Hall of Justice and informed them that "the Dahlia murder suspect was a doctor and we know who did it, but we couldn't put him away."

On August 15, 1967, some seventeen years after solving the Black Dahlia murder and locking his secret away in the DA vault, Frank Jemison died in Beverly Hills, California. He was sixty-eight.

He died a rich man. His will gave some of it to his alma mater, Wesleyan College in Ohio. The rest of his assets, after his wife Jane's death, were placed as a trust fund for the Los Angeles District Attorney's Office.

In 1979, the Frank Jemison Award was established from his bequest for the purpose of selecting and acknowledging "excellence in public service."

Every year since then, the award has been given to two outstanding employees selected from the DA's Office. One of the recipients is a DA investigator, and the other from the DA's support staff. Each Jemison Award Winner receives $5,000 cash.

DA INVESTIGATOR WALTER MORGAN—THE LAST COYOTE

"I guess there's not too many left in the hills in the city—least near where I live. So whenever I see one, I get this feeling that it might be the last one left out there. You know? The last coyote. And I guess that would bother me if it ever turned out to be true, if I never saw one again." —Detective Harry Bosch, from Michael Connelly's *The Last Coyote*

The following is based on an obituary I wrote for DA Investigator Walter Morgan when he died in 2007.

September 8, 2007
Los Angeles

DA INVESTIGATOR WALTER MORGAN,
BLACK DAHLIA MURDER'S LAST COYOTE DIES AT 92
1915-2007

Walter Morgan, the Los Angeles District Attorney's Bureau of Investigation "old school" detective and the last surviving member of the 1950 Black Dahlia DA Task Force, in the final years before his passing, linked Dr. George Hill Hodel to the 1947 murder.

In a 2004 CBS *48 Hours* crimespecial, Morgan publicly acknowledged bugging the doctor's private home. He also confirmed the existence of secret surveillance tapes and transcripts, and that the DA's 1950 task force was unexpectedly and summarily shut down. In a surprisingly candid on-air response, Morgan acknowledged that he and his fellow officers suspected that the shutdown was the result of a payoff and cover-up.

For me, it ended as it began with this morning's call from my half-sister, Tamar Hodel. "Steve, I just heard from my daughter, Fauna. Walter Morgan died this morning."

In my book, *Black Dahlia Avenger: A Genius for Murder,* published in 2003, here is how I originally described my introduction and first meeting with Walter Morgan, then an eighty-seven-year-old retired L.A. district attorney investigator.

Page 449:
My INVESTIGATION HAD BEEN COMPLETED for some four months. I was working on the final editing of the manuscript when on April 24, 2002, my phone rang. It was my sister Tamar. "Steven," she said, "I have the most amazing news. Fauna [her eldest daughter] has just spoken with a man named Walter Morgan." (I immediately recognized his name as a district attorney investigator, Lieutenant Jemison's partner from the 1950 investigation, and swallowed hard at hearing his name come from her lips.) "He was a private detective or something back in the 1940s," she said. "He was involved in investigating, guess who: *Dr. George Hodel!* He told Fauna that they put a bug in the Franklin House to listen in on Dad's conversations. Can you call Fauna and find out what this is all about?"

I assured Tamar I would check it out immediately. Contacting Fauna, whom I had not spoken to for ten years, I learned she was working in the San Fernando Valley and had been visited in her place of work by a casual acquaintance, Ethel. In her seventies, Ethel was with her boyfriend whom she introduced as Walter Morgan. Walter shook Fauna's hand and said, "'Hodel?' That's an unusual name. I once worked a murder case on a Dr. Hodel. Any relation?" Fauna and Walter compared notes, and quickly learned that Morgan's suspect and Fauna's grandfather were one and the same.

Two days later, on April 26, I called Walter Morgan and told him my name was Steven Hodel, the uncle of Fauna Hodel, and the son of Dr. George Hill Hodel, who had died in 1999 at the age of ninety-one. I also informed him that I had retired from LAPD after working most of my career as a homicide detective in Hollywood Division.

Morgan greeted me warmly, in that unspoken bond that exists cop to cop, and proceeded to reminisce about the Hodel story.

Morgan, now eighty-seven, said he had worked for the sheriff's department from 1939 to 1949 on radio car patrol, in vice, burglary, and in other details. Then he left LASD and became a DA investigator in 1949, where he remained until retirement in 1970. He worked homicide on temporary assignment for a few months back in 1950. He was sent over to help out Lieutenant Frank Jemison, who he said "had picked me to be his sidekick."

Walter Morgan remembered well the day they had installed listening devices at the Franklin House, which he authoritatively informed me "was built by Frank Lloyd Wright." (As we know, the true architect was his son, Lloyd Wright.) Morgan continued:

"We had a good bug man, a guy that could install bugs anywhere and everywhere. He worked in the DA's crime lab. So the chief assigned me to take him over to the house on Franklin, and he was going to install a bug system at the Hodel residence. My chief at the DA's office had me take him over there and we met the LAPD at Dr. Hodel's house. It was during the daytime and nobody was home. I remember there were some ranking LAPD officers outside, and no one could figure out how to get in. I suggested, "Well, have any of you officers tried a card to see if it would open the door?" They laughed, so I pulled out my wallet, and took out some kind of a credit card or whatever card I had, slipped it through, and the front door popped right open! They couldn't believe it. Anyway, our man went in and installed some bugs there. That was our job, to get the bugs installed so we could listen in."

Based on Walter Morgan's confirmations that my father was the Black Dahlia suspect and our Franklin house was bugged and secret tapes obtained, I closed the chapter (written in 2002) by publicly asking the following questions:

BDA page 454:
Standard operating procedure would have been to make transcripts of these conversations, as well as investigative follow-up reports documenting the findings. ***Where are these transcripts? Where are these reports? What do they say?***

A month after publication (May 2003), those questions were answered.

Los Angeles District Attorney Steve Cooley granted me access to the locked and vaulted *Hodel-Black Dahlia Files*, which had remained unexamined for over fifty-years, and, as they say, "the rest is history."

In June 2004, the five-decade-old surveillance transcripts and investigative reports, along with photographs and copies of the DA files, were released to the public by way of a new chapter, "Aftermath," added to the BDA's HarperCollins paperback edition.

DA LIEUTENANT WALTER MORGAN—BIOGRAPHY

- 1939- Appointed a deputy with the Los Angeles Sheriff's Department. Highly skilled in firearms, became one of the sheriff's department's "crack shots" after qualifying as a "Distinguished Expert" marksman.
- 1940-1949- L.A. deputy sheriff for nine years. Assignments included: patrol car, vice, and detective bureau (Burglary Detail).
- 1949- Left the sheriff's department and appointed a detective with the Los Angeles District Attorney's Office, Bureau of Investigation.
- 1950- Selected by Lt. Frank Jemison to assist him in the Grand Jury ordered reinvestigation of the Black Dahlia case.
- February 15, 1950- Morgan, ordered by Lt. Jemison to coordinate a meeting between DA crime lab electronics' expert and LAPD detectives for the specific purpose of surreptitiously installing microphones inside the Franklin house residence of Dr. George Hill Hodel. Morgan accompanied by "bug men" and "high ranking LAPD officers" proceeded to 5121 Franklin Avenue and personally "shimmed" the front door of Dr. Hodel's residence. [To prevent him from walking in on them, the "installation" was coordinated and done at the same time George Hodel was being detained for questioning by DA investigators at the Hall of Justice.]
- March 1970- Morgan retired from the DA's Office.
- April 2002- Interviewed by me about the Black Dahlia investigation and for the first time in fifty-two years, confirmed George Hodel as the prime suspect and the "bugging of the Hodel residence."
- May 2004- Interviewed on CBS *48 Hours*, where he publicly acknowledged that he "shimmed the front door" of Dr. Hodel's residence, and "electronic experts placed bugs in the walls." Morgan confirmed that he and Lt. Jemison were unexpectedly removed from the case and it was returned back to LAPD for further investigation. In an on-camera statement, Morgan indicated that in 1950, "a cover-up and payoff was suspected."
- September 8, 2007- Morgan fell ill and passed away in Los Angeles.

In several meetings with Walter Morgan after our introduction in 2002, I became acutely aware that he was a man of many moods and many secrets, most of them from a long time ago.

In his prime, Morgan lived and breathed *Chinatown* and *LA Confidential*. He *was L.A. noir*—only this gumshoe was no celluloid fiction—he was the real deal. As you will read below, he was Philip Marlowe (before Marlowe got fired from the DA's Office for insubordination) and Dirty Harry rolled into one. And in 1944, a couple of street thugs would "make his day."

In the mid-1940s, Morgan was close to the power that influenced and ran Los Angeles: gangster Mickey Cohen, Florentine Gardens' owner Mark Hansen, and his "Mr. Show Business," M.C. Nils Thor Granlund, better known as-"N.T.G."

In 1945, Morgan married the Florentine's lead showgirl, Tanya "Sugar" Geise. Best man at his wedding was no less a luminary, than L.A. County's top-cop, Sheriff Eugene Biscailuz. Tanya was good friends with Lavonne Cohen, Mickey Cohen's wife, who also attended the wedding. Mickey Cohen was Bugsy Siegel's lieutenant who, in two short years, would take over as L.A.'s *Numero Uno* gangster after his boss was gunned down in Beverly Hills.

Below I've included just a few press clippings from Morgan's Feisty Forties, to give a sense of the man in his time.

In 1944, while still a deputy sheriff, Morgan was parked in a car with his fiancée Sugar Geise on the Sunset Strip. The couple was approached by two armed robbers.

Excerpt from L.A. *Times* article on September 30, 1944:

Dead-Shot Deputy Foils Two Asserted Bandits

...
Suddenly one of them (Gallentine) shoved a pistol through a partly open window, rapped on the glass, and said, "O.K., give us the dough and the jewels"

Let "Jewels" Go

"I (Morgan) stepped out and said, "O.K., here are your jewels—and let go eight 'little jewels' from my automatic."

Florentine Gardens Showgirl Tanya "Sugar" Geise

June 8, 1945 Los Angeles Times

Sugar Geise Wed to Deputy Sheriff

Dep. Sheriff Walter Morgan and Tanya (Sugar) Geise, Florentine Gardens night-club singer, whom he once saved from two bandits, yesterday were married in Superior Judge Edward R. Brand's court chambers.

Best man at the double-ring ceremony was Sheriff Biscailuz, with Mrs. Sam Katzman, wife of the R.K.O. producer, acting as matron of honor.

The couple met two years ago while Miss Geise was the star attraction at the Florentine Gardens. Last September, while Morgan was escorting her home, two bandits attempted to hold them up. Morgan leaped from the automobile and wounded both men in a blazing gun battle. Later they were convicted of robbery and sentenced to San Quentin.

"That convinced me I had met the right guy," Sugar declared yesterday after the wedding. She gave her age as 28 and Morgan admitted to being 30.

Other attendants at the wedding were Sugar's father, Harry (Pop) Geise, Lt. John Law, Morgan's immediate superior officer,

and Mrs. Lillian Cohen and Miss Pauline Davis, friends of the bride.

Immediately after the ceremony the couple left for a honeymoon trip which will include San Francisco and Reno.

THREE'S A CROWD—Dep. Sheriff Walter Morgan, about to kiss his bride, Tanya (Sugar) Geise, night club singer, following wedding ceremony yesterday, apparently intends to push Sheriff Biscailuz, best man, out of picture.

Times photo

Walter Morgan weds Sugar Geise in June 1945, Sheriff Biscailuz "Best Man"

2004- 48 Hours Black Dahlia Confidential

CBS investigative reporter Erin Moriarty questions Walter Morgan regarding the Black Dahlia case being closed down and turned back to LAPD

Morgan: The only thing I can think is that some money must have transpired between people.

Moriarty: It sounds like you think it may have been a cover-up of some sort?

Morgan: Well, everybody thought that.

Dr. George Hill Hodel Surveillance Transcripts 40 days--(146 pages)

To DA investigators Frank Jemison and Walter Morgan: I want to personally thank both of you for your service to the City of Angels and its people. Thank you for your honesty and integrity. You did what others could not. One of you preserved the truth and the other told it.

May you both rest in peace.

DA investigator Walter Morgan in 1952 walking across the street from his office at the Hall of Justice. [Federal Court in background.]

LAPD/LASD/DA – "DAHLIA CASE WAS SOLVED" – THEN

"We identified the Black Dahlia suspect. He was a doctor."

William H. Parker
LAPD Chief of Police

"The Black Dahlia case was solved. He was a doctor who lived on Franklin Avenue in Hollywood. "

Thad Brown
LAPD Chief of Detectives

"We know who the Black Dahlia killer was. He was a doctor, but we didn't have enough to put him away.

Lt. Frank B. Jemison
DA Bureau of Investigation

"The Black Dahlia Case was solved., but it will never come out. The suspect was a doctor they all knew in Hollywood, involved in abortions."

Undersheriff James Downey to J. Gordon Bowers, Chief of Detectives
Los Angeles Sheriff's Dept

NOW

2004-- LAPD & LASO COMMANDERS & HEAD DEPUTY DA INDEPENDENTLY OPINE "BLACK DAHLIA CASE SOLVED"

"The hardcover book was pretty compelling. Then when all the transcripts and stuff came out from the D.A.'s Office, that took it over the top for me. That would have been enough for me to bring a case against Dr. Hodel."
L. A. Times Magazine, Nov. 21, 2004

"In 1962 I was a detective and I was the driver for Undersheriff James Downey who was the Sheriff Dept's #2 man... One day he was going to lunch with his good friend, Gordy Bowers, Chief of Detectives. Somehow the Black Dahlia murder case came up in conversation. I heard Jimmy say, "Oh, that had been solved, but it will never come out. It was some doctor they all knew out in Hollywood."
In my own professional opinion Hodel has put the pieces together and solved the case."
CBS Television Interview Oct. 2004

LAPD Deputy Chief James McMurray (ret.)
Chief of Detectives

LASO Cmdr. Thomas Vetter (ret.)
Lt. Col. USMC (ret.)

" Steve (Hodel) has taken this way beyond the pictures. It no longer depends on the pictures."
L. A. Times Magazine, Nov. 21, 2004

"I have no doubt in my mind that George Hodel murdered Elizabeth Short.... If the witnesses were alive today, I believe if I took that case in front of a jury, that I would convict him."
Rue 13, French television documentary, The Truth About The Black Dahlia Nov. 6, 2006

LA Head Dep. DA Stephen Kay (ret.)

"...I actually agree with you, I think he [Hodel] has made a very compelling theory. I think there's a lot of things that looks like it and his dad could actually be responsible for the murder of the Black Dahlia."

--LAPD Detective II Mitzi Roberts
KMEX Television interview, La Dahlia Negra
April, 2013

"Unless you find some major holes in Hodel's investigation, go ahead and clear the Black Dahlia case."

Dep. Chief James McMurray
LAPD Chief of Detectives

ABOUT THE AUTHOR

Steve Hodel was born and brought up in Los Angeles. Now a private investigator, he spent almost twenty-four years with the LAPD, most of them as a homicide detective-supervisor. During his tenure, he worked on more than three hundred murder cases, and had one of the highest "solve rates" on the force. He currently resides in the Los Angeles area. *Black Dahlia Avenger: A Genius for Murder,* published in 2003, became a *New York Times* bestseller.

Steve's Black Dahlia investigation and related books have been featured as full-hour segments on: *Dateline NBC, CBS 48-Hours, A&E Bill Kurtis Cold Case Files, Discovery Channel "Most Evil"* and *The Truth about the Black Dahlia on NBC Universal (France)*

Visit his Web site at www.stevehodel.com

OTHER BOOKS BY STEVE HODEL:

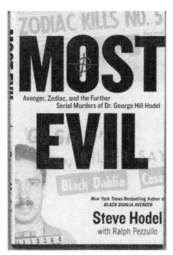

For more information, visit:
www.stevehodel.com
www.blog.stevehodel.com

THICKER'N THIEVES

THE 1950 FACTUAL EXPOSE OF POLICE PAY-OFFS, GRAFT,
POLITICAL CORRUPTION AND PROSTITUTION IN
LOS ANGELES AND HOLLYWOOD

by
SGT. CHARLES STOKER
EX-LAPD VICE-SQUAD OFFICER

Foreword by Steve Hodel

LAPD Hollywood Homicide Detective (ret.)
New York Times Bestselling Author of *Black Dahlia Avenger*

Printed in Great Britain
by Amazon